# The
# Palestinians

*People of the Olive Tree*

# The
# Palestinians

*People of the Olive Tree*

Dr. Kamel S. Abu Jaber

HESPERUS

Published by Hesperus Press Limited

www.hesperus.press

*The Palestinians: People of the Olive Tree* © Kamel S. Abu Jaber 2021

Kamel S. Abu Jaber asserts his moral right to be identified as the author of
this work under the Copyright, Designs and Patents Act 1988.

Photographs courtesy of United Nations Relief and Works Agency for
Palestine Refugees in the Near East © UNRWA ARCHIVES

First Published by Jordan Book Center, 1995

Second Edition Published by Hesperus Press Limited, 2021

Designed and typeset by Roland Codd

ISBN 978-1-84391-985-8

ebook ISBN 978-1-84391-986-5

*For the Palestinians*
*&*
*The innocent victims of conflicts in
the Middle East*

In remembrance of H.E. Dr. Kamel Saleh Abu Jaber

1932–2020

For his dedication to higher education, to peace building in the Middle East, the promotion of peaceful coexistence among nations, and his great contribution to understanding the Arab world in all its intricacies; he has left a lasting legacy.

His kind smile, his sense of humor, his zest for life that kept him eternally young, his positive impact on all those he met are sorely missed.

He was a truly special man. I am blessed to have had the pleasure of sharing his beautiful life.

Of his numerous works in English, I have chosen to republish the following books: *The Arab Ba'ath Socialist Party: History, Ideology and Organization*, (Syracuse University Press, 1966); *The Jordanians and the People of Jordan* (Royal Scientific Society, Jordan, 1980); *Sheepland* (Hesperus Press, 2005); *The Palestinians: People of the Olive Tree* (Jordan Book Centre Co., 1995).

*Loretta Abjalen*

Loretta Pacifico Abu Jaber
Devoted and loving wife of 62 years

# Contents

# Preface

Palestine and its indigenous Arab population have become part of a short phrase, "the Palestine problem". The Holy Land made sacrosanct by the three great monotheistic Abrahamic religions – Judaism, Christianity and Islam – is now, once again, besieged by violence and strife. Moses only looked at it from across the Jordan River; Jesus lived and died in it; while Mohammad [pbuh] venerated and respected it, and his *isra* – nocturnal journey from Holy Mecca to Holy Jerusalem – gave it further significance. To this day, the Arabs of the land identify people by religion: Musawi, 'Issawi and Mohammadan; followers of Moses, Jesus and Mohammad, respectively.

The essays, events and stories presented here are not meant to catalogue Palestine's history or trace the progress of the modern Palestine problem. It is hoped that they capture the spirit of a proud and peaceful people. Ancient residents of the land, the Palestinians find themselves humbled by forces they cannot understand, and by hatreds they can neither understand nor fathom.

The stories in the following pages are chronologically accurate; hopefully they will capture the feelings at the time. They are a mirror reflecting the inner thoughts and feelings of a once peaceful people suddenly subjected to sustained abuse of limitless dimensions. For, the Palestinians feel hunted, wherever on earth they happen to be, and witness their historical record, as cities, towns and villages are razed to the ground, erased from the face of the earth to make way for Zionist colonies and settlements; their soul and land distorted to accommodate someone else's myth. But even if sometimes they feel overwhelmed, they cling to the resolve to defend themselves, their identity, their land and their culture. They feel alienated for they do not think they truly belong anywhere except on their own land, which is now inhabited by someone else.

The intensity of emotion contained in these essays and stories must surely be viewed as a reaction to the terrible reality of the life led by most Palestinians, wherever they may be. The stories were selected from among the many told to me. Every Palestinian has a different story, but underneath appears a central theme. That is what I looked for. I have attempted to articulate to the non-Arab reader the inner sentiments and thoughts of the Palestinian people who have been cruelly and unjustly treated, and often deliberately misunderstood. In modern times, life has not been easy for most of the Arab world. For the Palestinians, it has been a terrible and continuous nightmare. That is why I urge the reader to read this book in more than one sitting.

At one time or another, every Arab, indeed every Muslim, becomes an ardent Palestinian – not only out of a sense of human solidarity against the injustice done to the Palestinians, or from a sense of outrage against the Western conspiracy of silence and duplicity, but also, and more importantly, because of the centrality of Jerusalem and Palestine in Arab and Muslim life.

I wrote the introductory historical background chapter to describe how a young Palestinian views his past and present while agonizing over his future. In the stories that follow, I only recount what was told to me.

Kamel S. Abu Jaber

# Introduction

## Historical Ironies

The Palestinians – who are they? To their neighbors, the Jordanians, they were the people who lived across the Jordan River. Today, no one knows exactly where the Palestinians are or how many there are. Are they a political entity? Most of the world recognizes the PLO and now their state, which still exists more in their heart than anywhere else. Or are they simply a 'social' group that happens to exist on the margins of regional and world affairs? The Zionists and their allies deny their existence, claiming they are a nonentity. Yet, if that is so, who are those people residing in the refugee camps of Jordan, Syria, Lebanon and elsewhere? Who are those people fighting to free their land and training for the day of deliverance and return, their Intifada a symbol of dignity for free men everywhere? Are they ghosts? And, if so, how come they are taken so seriously? Or have the Zionists and their allies lost so much touch with reality that they became modern-day Don Quixotes? To what purpose have the Palestinians been reduced to nonentities, non-persons, brutalized and dehumanized? And how is it that the Western newspaperman, diplomat, or politician at once denies the existence of the Palestinians and demands that they be contained? Or is it easier on the conscience to commit cruelty against someone that is abstracted from reality?

The Palestinians still exist. Some of them live on their own land, denied recognition elsewhere and subjected to the mental and physical cruelty of the Zionist organization, whose tentacles reach deep. The Zionist organization came into existence to alleviate injustices committed by the West against Jews, but now it metes out similar and often more severe atrocities against the hapless Palestinians. Now the Palestinians, too, are learning the necessary lessons for survival in modern times. The learning process may seem slow, but the manual from which they are learning, the Zionist manual, is thorough and meticulous.

The Zionist movement was created in Basel, Switzerland, in 1897 by a Viennese newspaperman named Theodor Herzl, and was to oust the Palestinians from their ancestral homes in Palestine some 50 years later. Herzl was incensed, and rightly so, about the "unjudicial" treatment of a captain in the French army called Alfred Dreyfus. Unfortunately for the Palestinians then, and 50 years later, that French captain happened to be Jewish, and because he was Jewish, his was not a trial but a miscarriage of justice. The French courts, blinded by anti-Semitic public opinion, through a trial attended by a Viennese journalist, caused the Palestinians to become strangers in their own land. For, today, in the land across the river from the Hashemite Kingdom of Jordan, is a created country called Israel. It is inhabited by some of our cousins, the Jews, and many Poles, Germans, Russians, Americans and others whose religion happens to be Jewish.

Some Palestinians, though they do not dare call themselves that, still remain on this land. Though treated as second-class subjects, they patiently hope for the day when this injustice shall pass; for the day when they can walk freely on their land and develop their country. Despite all the attempts to make them forget, they do not, for the holy river – The Jordan – runs in their veins; in their mind's eye, they can visualize their past on its banks. Their land has witnessed the use of clay, bronze and iron; a procession of prophets, soothsayers, tyrants and liberators; and the birth of ideas, ideologies and religions. There are settlements and landmarks by the hundreds to remind them of their past. Ismael Ibn Ibrahim, brother of Ishaq [Isaac], is among their ancestors, and Ya'qoub [Jacob], who was in love with Leah, still has his well in Nablus, in that part of Palestine now called the West Bank. It, too, is now under Israeli occupation.

## Alfred Dreyfus and Theodor Herzl

Who was Dreyfus and what is his story? How did the fate of that unfortunate French soldier come to affect the lives and fortunes of so many millions of his co-religionists, of the Palestinians and, indeed, of humanity?

In 1894, it became common knowledge that an officer of the French General Staff had been selling military secrets to the Germans. Captain Alfred Dreyfus was the only Jew on the staff, and though his record as a soldier was honorable, he was selected as a convenient scapegoat. The actual traitor was protected while Dreyfus was vilified. His condemnation to serve a prison term on Devil's Island was the culmination of a classic case of miscarriage of justice. The trial proceedings were attended by Theodor Herzl, reporting for the Viennese newspaper *Neue Freie Presse*. The conviction and public degradation of this good officer were accompanied by a severe outburst of anti-Semitic sentiment. Emile Zola, the famous French novelist, was so moved by the gross injustice that he wrote a letter to the French newspapers titled "J'accuse". In the letter, he indicted France for its "crime against humanity". Through the efforts of Zola and Georges Clemenceau, Dreyfus was retried in 1899, and again condemned, but public opinion had been aroused by then, and on 19 September 1899 he was pardoned. Later, proof of innocence led to his complete exoneration in 1906 and the restoration to his rank in the army. To the end, Dreyfus was a French patriot who regarded his conviction as a mistake. He was never fully aware of the wider implications of his case. During World War I, he served as a lieutenant-colonel in the French army.

Herzl was greatly moved by the violent anti-Semitic passions aroused by the Dreyfus trial. As a young intellectual, he had been more interested in Jewish assimilation, not nationalism. To that end, he even toyed with the idea of mass Jewish conversion to Christianity. His chance attendance at the Dreyfus trial caused him to reconsider his position. From then on, he began to argue that the Jewish problem could not be solved except by recognition of the Jews as a nation. He explained his new ideas in a concise booklet titled *The Jewish State*.

The conception of a state for the Jews, baptized in French anti-Semitism in the late nineteenth century and with the help of British imperial interests bore fruit in the twentieth century. Adolf Hitler, another Viennese, aroused another ugly storm of anti-Semitism that finally brought about the birth of Israel. Neither conception nor birth was immaculate. Was Herzl's conversion to nationalism an historical accident? Had he not attended Dreyfus' ordeal, would he have developed his ideas? Who knows for sure? Did Herzl not visualize the agony his articulation of Jewish nationalism would have on the Palestinians? But then Zionism is older than Herzl and it is also possible that it would have found expression through someone else, albeit in a different form. It is certain, though, that very few Palestinians know of Captain Dreyfus and his ordeal, or of Herzl's conversion to Zionism.

## Denial of the Palestinians

"What are the Palestinians? When I came here there were only 250,000 non-Jews, mainly Arabs and Bedouins," the then Israeli prime minister, Levi Eshkol, said in the Israeli newspaper *Davar*, on 24 January 1969. Eshkol was Russian, so he might be pardoned for not knowing, or pretending not to know, that Palestinians are Arabs and some of them are Bedouins. Golda Myerson [Meir], originally an American, said later in the same year: "There were no such things as Palestinians ... It was not as though there was a Palestinian people in Palestine considering itself as a Palestinian people, and we came and threw them out and took their country away from them. They did not exist."

That is how successive Israeli prime ministers preferred to deny the existence of the Palestinians. Eshkol said there were Arabs and Bedouins, without using the term Palestinians, while Meir denies their existence altogether. Who, then, were the people exterminated in Deir Yasin by Menachem Begin's terrorist organization in 1948, and by Yitzhak Shamir following the Palestinian Intifada of 1987?

One of the most important problems facing us, Arabs, in dealing with Zionists is that they seem to be less logical in their thinking than we are. George Steiner, author, critic and fellow of Churchill College at Cambridge University, stated at the Sixth American-Israeli Dialogue held in Jerusalem in 1968: "The existence of Israel is not founded on logic. It has no ordinary legitimacy. There is neither in its establishment nor present scope any evident justice."

But then, who listens to logic or cares about justice when the slogan "might makes right" reigns supreme? But I digress. The fates of Palestinians and Jews are so intertwined that one cannot speak about one people without reference to the other.

The Palestinians – who constituted at least 93 per cent of the population of Palestine in 1917 when the Balfour Declaration was issued, and even today, after so many forced migrations, still constitute a sizeable group in Palestine – are ignored and denied existence. In 1993, there remain on the land of Palestine an estimated 2.3 million Palestinians, who are denied political and civil rights, and though they suffer humiliation, discrimination and indignity, they continue to cling to their land, to their ancestral home and to hope. Palestinians still hope that some accommodation with the "cousins" of the Arabs can be worked out before it is too late, and that the latter-day injustice inflicted on them will pass in spite of the atrocities, the breaking of bones and souls, the daily murders and the denial of the most elementary human rights. By contrast, even the treatment of the blacks in South Africa seems humane.

## Historical Echoes

The Palestinians' memory is long, almost as long as their history. As a Middle Eastern social group, their land always contained a mixture of groups, nationalities, languages, religions and creeds. When Islam came, it blessed and sanctioned an already existing tolerance – an acceptance of other peoples, groups and religions. From the study of human remains, anthropologists found that 50,000 years ago, the Palestinians were already a mixed racial group. From the fourth millennium to about 900 BC, the predominant indigenous group was the Canaanites, ancestors of the Arabs. Palestine got its name from the sea people, the Philistines, who occupied its southern coast in the twelfth century BC, at about the same time the Hebrews arrived. Since then, and perhaps like very few other countries, Palestine has witnessed a slew of civilizations arriving and departing, each leaving a mark on the land and on its people. Nearly every mountain or bend in any road has witnessed some great historical event or prophesy.

After the Canaanites came the Egyptian Pharaohs, then the Hittites, and then a combination of Canaanites, Philistines and Hebrews. Next came the Babylonians, followed by the Persians, Greeks, Ptolemies, Seleucids, Maccabees, Seleucids again, and then Romans. The Persians returned, as did the Romans, then the Arabs arrived with Islam, then the

Turks came followed by the Crusaders, the Egyptians, the Mamelukes, the Ottomans, the British and now the Israeli Jews. It is a huge succession of civilizations covering about 6,000 years of human existence. The people underneath all these civilizations, the Palestinians, have always been there, in their land. The face of the conqueror may have changed, but they always knew that the land underneath is Palestine.

Hardly a Palestinian is unaware of at least some aspect of this past. Some, busying themselves with the problems of their daily life in Toronto, Canada; Sidney, Australia; or downtown Amman, Jordan, try to forget. But few do. For the lure of Palestine and its image as home – land of milk and honey, prophets and religions – is not easy to forget. It is imprinted on the subconscious of the child before its birth. You see, there is such beauty and pride in being a Palestinian. The Arabs, too, are from the seed of *Sayyidnah*[1] Ibrahim [Abraham], in Arabic called *al-Khalil, Khalilulah,* friend of God. Many of their ancestors knew the prophets personally. They consorted with Amos, Jeremiah, Miccah, Josea, the two Isaiahs, Elijah, the Judges, the Psalmists, Job, and Jonah. Some of their ancestors listened to *Yasu'al-Nasiri,* Jesus of Nazareth, and to his Apostles, Paul, Peter, John, Luke, Mark and Matthew. Mohammed Ibn Abdullah [pbuh] blessed Jerusalem and the lands around it. He made Jerusalem his first *qiblah*, direction of the prayer for the faithful. Jerusalem was so revered in the Islamic era that no Muslim ruler ever attempted to make it the political capital of his reign.

---

1. An Arabic term of respect for a Prophet

Jerusalem, the Flower of Cities; Shekim, Shechem [Nablus], housing the Samaritan temple; Al-Khalil [Hebron], housing the remains of Sarah; Ariha, [Jericho], whose walls tumbled down at the sound of Joshua's trumpets; Lake Galilee, Tiberias, where Jesus walked on its water; Cana, where Jesus attended a wedding and performed his first miracle, the conversion of water into wine; Al-Nasirah [Nazareth], the ancient beauty; and Beit Lahim [Bethlehem], birthplace of Jesus; Jaffa, Askalan, Mlabbis, Acca [Acre], that repulsed Napoleon's siege, and fair Haifa with Mount Carmel overlooking the beautiful Mediterranean; Meggido, Beitshan or Beisan, Beit Jala, al-Aizriah, and hundreds of other hamlets, towns, *tels, wadis,* and landmarks, are all witnesses of civilizations of older times. The memory is so stretched it cannot seem to absorb the span of time, civilizations or personalities.

And then, Lake Huleh was dried up by the Israeli authorities, and the waters of the holy Jordan River diverted to irrigate lands to grow vegetables in the Negev desert – the Jordan River that gave its name to the lands lying east of it while the people, the Palestinians, gave their name to the land west of it. Can all this history, this memory, be forgotten simply because Eshkol or Meir or Shamir deny the existence of the Palestinians? Just remember how the Caliph Omar Ibn al-Khattab entered Jerusalem: a lone camel-rider with a companion advancing to its walls. Archbishop Sofronius of Jerusalem, an Arab from Damascus, hardly believed his eyes: "Is this the mighty Caliph Omar walking or riding? Where are his armies?" The story Palestinian children recall is that, peacefully, he entered the city and was greeted by its people.

In fact, the story goes that he was leading the camel, it being the turn of his servant to ride.

The Caliph toured the city and then visited the Church of the Holy Sepulchre and while he was inside, it was time for the 'asr, mid-afternoon, prayer. The Caliph asked where he could pray and the Archbishop asked: "Why don't you pray right here?" The Caliph, aware that later generations might convert the place into a mosque, refused and went outside and performed his prayers opposite the church. On that very place was built a small mosque that still exists. Later, another caliph, Salah al-Din, known in the West as Saladdin, set yet another precedent that has survived till now. The many Christian denominations within the Church of the Holy Sepulchre were always at odds as to who should have the privilege of keeping the keys to the gates of the church. They turned to the caliph and the patriarch, who suggested a neutral party; the keys have since been kept in the hands of the Nusseibehs, a Muslim Jerusalemite family. Later, during Salah al-Din's reign, further division of labor took place. The Nusseibeh family kept the privilege of opening the gates, while the privilege of closing them in the evening was given to another Muslim family, the Judehs of Jerusalem, a privilege they too have kept till the present.

## Palestinian Memory

For the Palestinians who still remember Palestine, and all do, even those born elsewhere and who never saw it, it is painful to recall how it was. Many of them often leave their homes in Amman, or their huts or tents in the close-by Bak'a camp, near Amman, for the hills of Mahis and Fuheis overlooking the Jordan Valley. For, in the early evening, they can see the Jordan River valley, the Dead Sea and above it the mountains of Palestine on the other side of the river. When it gets dark, they can see some of the lights of Jerusalem twinkling in the distance like a mirage, a dream that is beyond grasp.

"Write this in your book," said Mahmoud Darwish, a young Palestinian poet. "Jerusalem is under occupation and Arabs, Muslims or Christians, Jordanians, Palestinians or Syrians cannot enter it without … without what? … The old Palestinians, whose faces are lined with time, remember how it was: a land good to them. Generous land, whose holy earth, though mountainous, was giving and open. Since the dawn of time it has been known as the land of milk and honey. It was never a desert made to bloom by latter-day Zionists."

The young Palestinians, in their camps on cold winter nights, huddled together under blankets, several in the space ordinarily enough for one person, listen to how it was. They are the people of the olive tree, hardy and with a long memory. The memory is transmitted to them and they sing songs about their return. In their hearts they know their return is inevitable, yet they do not enjoy the waiting, or the struggle. They too are a peaceful people. Like their brothers and neighbors across the Jordan River, and like most other Arabs, they too are compromisers and peacemakers. They too remember Issa's [Jesus'] injunction, "Blessed are the peacemakers." They are not apologetic about Abu Ammar's [Yasir Arafat's] stance at the United Nations, a rifle in one hand and an olive branch in the other. They would rather have peace, but they insist it should be honorable and just. For these young Palestinians, children of the muddy camps in Jordan, Syria, Lebanon or elsewhere, often denounced by the Western media as terrorists, Palestine has become an ideal. Though many of them have never seen it, it has been imprinted on their minds, a recurring dream, passionate and sweet, of how things could have been. It has become a kingdom in their hearts, and like a religious litany, their souls swear to return to a homeland most have only heard about. The desperation of the fathers is communicated to and inherited by the sons who vow that one day they will return.

These young Palestinians, like all young Arabs, watch with fascination and incomprehension a world that continues to misunderstand them. Not only are they not understood, but also no one seems to really care. They watch the parade of visitors to their camps with false hope, for they have been studied, interrogated, screened, scrutinized, pictured, polled, and polled again, so many times they cannot even recall. American professors and journalists are followed by senators, congressmen, women's leaders, labor leaders, military commanders, French newspapermen, Dutch Orientalists, German municipal delegations, Belgian bureaucrats, Swedish technocrats and even Eastern autocrats. Norwegian philanthropists are followed by British members of parliament, Italian survey teams, and Spanish parliamentarians. No sooner has one delegation left than it is followed by a procession of others. The Palestinians, young and old, feel they have been dissected, autopsied, studied, X-rayed so many times they have stopped counting. Organizations, clubs, associations, institutions, foundations, scientific societies follow each other in such huge succession that the color, smell and tone have merged to form one nasty reality of desperation and frustration. Yet the elders dutifully don their best clothes, maintain their dignity and turn out each time to repeat what they said the time before, the day before, 16 September 1962, or 1958 or 1952.

The young watch with fascinated impatience. No one is protecting them from the elements, physical or mental. Day in and day out they are bombarded with the accusation that they are terrorists. Abroad, they feel hunted and taunted. It has become something odious and nasty to be a Palestinian. Abroad, many of them, to ward off an often-repeated argument, keep quiet about their identity. They watch their history and the history of their land written and rewritten in the Zionist image and they watch the Arab "giant", huge yet prostrate and unable to defend itself, let alone regain Palestine. Why, they ask? Why are we so helpless when we seem to have so much? Where is our leadership? Where is our past? Where is our future? Why are our affairs so ineptly handled? Why does no one understand us? Are we really so illogical and contradictory, or are we being deliberately misunderstood? How did we descend so far into the abyss, into this quagmire?

## The Jews and the Palestinians

The Palestinian people, numbering now around 5.5 million[7], are scattered throughout the world. The diaspora of the

7. Figure related to 1990s

Palestinian people was not an historic accident, nor was it the work of a tyrannical potentate in the dark ages. It was done in the light of day and in the middle of the twentieth century. The "civilized powers" that created the League of Nations in the 1920s judged that the Palestinians were not mature enough to govern themselves! And so it was that "civilized" Britain was awarded the mandate over Palestine. Lord Balfour, an Englishman, wrote a letter to Lord Rothschild, his compatriot, in which he promised an Arab land belonging to the Palestinians to a third party composed of many nationalities who happened to be Jewish. Let me quote A.M. Lilienthal in his monumental work, *The Zionist Connection* [New York, 1978, pp. 731-2, passim]: "Aside from the fact that the land for more than nineteen centuries has been inhabited overwhelmingly by Arabs, is Israel in fact the homeland of Herzl, Weizmann, Ben-Gurion, Meir, Rabin, Begin and Bellow as they have unhesitatingly … maintained?"

Arthur Koestler answers this question with an emphatic "No". In his 1976 best seller, *The Thirteenth Tribe,* the author dropped a bombshell by proving that today's European Jews were, for the most part, descendants of the Khazars, who converted to Judaism seven centuries after the destruction of Jerusalem, in 70 AD, and the dispersion of the small original Judaic Palestine population by the Roman Emperor Vespasian and his son Titus. The Khazars, a semi-nomadic Turko-Finnish people, who settled in what is now southern Russia, between the Volga and the Don, spread to the shores of the Black, Caspian and Azov seas. Jews who had been banished from Constantinople by Byzantine ruler Leo III found a home among the pagan Khazars and then, in competition with Muslim and Christian missionaries, won Khagan Bulan, the ruler of Khazaria, over to the Judaic faith around 740 AD. His nobles followed suit, and somewhat later so did his people. Some details of these events are contained in letters exchanged between Khagan [king] Joseph of Khazaria and Hasdai Ibn Shaprut of Cordova, doctor and quasi-foreign minister to Emir Abd al-Rahman III, the Umayyad Caliph of Cordova. When the Khazaria Empire was collapsing, its population of Jewish converts – Khazars – fled northwest to become the progenitors of Ashkenazim [Russian/German/Baltic/Polish] Jewry. Thus, the great majority of Eastern European Jews are not Semitic Jews at all.

But then who reads history accurately, especially when passion overshadows reason? And it is thus that the Palestinian Arabs, the true seed of Abraham, are now replaced by others. With impotent horror they were made to lie still while their land, their olive trees and groves were given to others. The British, the French and later the Americans were to arm, train and support the Zionists. And while talking to the Arabs, the Palestinians, they ignore them at the same time. When Menachem Begin said, "we fight therefore we are", they listened; when Arafat spoke of compromise, with an olive branch in his hand, he was called a terrorist. So termed are the hundreds of Palestinian youth. But those who trained for months for an airline hijack operation could not, in the end, kill innocents. When ultimately faced with that decision they chose to give themselves up. Parents watch their children hardening each day. They shake their heads in puzzlement as they read about and listen to their children being vilified and called terrorists. They ask why? And who made them so?

The Palestinians, indeed the Arabs, cannot break through the moral and mental barrier the Zionists built around the West. It is a curtain much stronger than any material hitherto known to man, a curtain erected to keep out truth, understanding, sympathy or justice. A curtain constructed from a barrage of propaganda bombarding the West with half-truths, false images and innuendo, with hatred, myth and illusion to create ugly new realities.

And so it was that the Palestinians of Palestine, the hosts of civilizations untold, were vilified. The peaceful people of the villages and hamlets of Palestine, who for thousands of years received foreigners with a smile, were made refugees, residents in temporary camps, victims of an international injustice of unparalleled proportions, and recipients of a meager international dole that has been dwindling with the passage of time. They do not know what happened to their homes, and their olive trees have been uprooted by Israeli bulldozers.


## Palestinian Bewilderment

Who should the Palestinians turn to? Where should they go?

In the Arab world, they find themselves pawns in the hands of this or that regime. Their acceptance by any given regime depends on the mood of the leader. To gain credence, many Arab leaders make frequent references to Palestine, often couched in an attack on Israel. Few mean what they say. Verbally, all the leaders and their peoples profess their love of Palestinians and pledge the most sacred oaths to liberate Palestine. On occasion, the earth shakes from the vehemence of rhetoric that often benefits Israel alone. Zionist propaganda, now aware of the "Arab game", often goads some Arab leader into issuing an extremely radical verbal attack. The more extreme and bellicose such an attack the better it is, for, on the strength of it, millions of dollars, marks or francs are solicited to help Israel against the belligerent Arabs.

Sometimes I wish the Arabs kept quiet about the Palestine problem for 10 or 20 years, until such time as it can be dealt with at least semi-efficiently. Verbal attacks by Arab leaders, no matter how justifiably provoked, serve only to help increase donations, and generate sympathy, both official and non-official, for Israel. They do no good at all for the Palestinians. In no Arab country are the Palestinians able to work freely to regain their land. Palestinians are merely used by one regime to gain advantage over another. In most Arab countries, the Palestinians are extolled yet viewed with suspicion. In many Arab countries, it is certain that Frenchmen, Italians or even Chinese residents or tourists are better off. Feared, loved or hated, used, bought, sold or abused, they are never allowed to wander too far from the limits of the strings which tie them to one Arab government or another. And when they lash out in anger, as they sometimes do, they are quickly and efficiently punished or contained.

They have grown to be suspicious, cynical, skeptical and frustrated. For, they are aware of the double-talk, the empty and rarely kept promises. While they and their children run the hospitals, businesses, factories and educational institutions in many Arab countries, they are given but token decision-making posts. Everywhere they are constantly scrutinized. People tell them they belong while glancing sidelong at each other with suspicion and fear. That is why they have learned to calculate every move, indeed every word. Their traditional open-mindedness and acceptance of ideas, peoples, religions and nationalities is now crowded to the extreme. Who can they trust?

Forty years of crisis have made them suspicious and cautious. They cannot depend on anything or anyone except themselves. Yet even that is proving more difficult with the passage of time, and their scattered residences, complex loyalties and creeping despair. They sometimes prefer to "let us wait and see", but that is not really an intrinsic trait of theirs. When they do sometimes choose, the choice is always between two evils. They have learned to become attuned to the moods of others and to live with those moods rather than their own. Before one storm has passed another always seems to loom on the horizon and each time they are weighed down with anger, bewilderment and frustration. The talk of their friends and brethren never seems to equal their actions. To them it seems as if the Arab mind has become detached from its body, for, the actions or reactions, if any, never seem to be directed by what the tongue says.

And it is thus that the Palestinians, slowly but ever so surely, turn inward. Once they were told to value their honor before anything else and yet, when they found themselves in tents and hovels, no one seemed to worry any more about their honor. In fact, often they hear statements of how they lost their land or even sold it to the Jews. And so each year they get buried under still more stacks of frustration and anger.

Sometimes I wonder how some of them can even smile. But they do, proving once again their resilience and their patient determination, a determination that helps them look forward to the future with hope. Is that why they have come to value education beyond almost everything else? I wonder. For, the Palestinians surely must have learned early the lesson that education means progress and living in accord with the times; that education, though not often bringing wealth or power, always brings dignity and awareness; that it links the present with the tools and technology of contemporary modern society; that education is wealth they can carry with them; that education links the past with the future. That is how they cling to some of their cherished values: an attachment and love for their land and its olive groves and orange and lemon orchards. Unlike the Jews, who are attached to Palestine to escape prejudice, for the Palestinians, the attachment is to the earth itself, to home. Perhaps that is why so many Palestinians bear the name of the village or town they came from as a family name. Witness the names: *al-Maqdisi*, Jerusalemite; *al-Yazuri*, Yazurite; *al-Bajjali* of Beit –Jala; *al-Nabulsi* of Nablus; *al-Yafawi* of Jaffa; *al-Nasiri*, Nazarine of Nazareth; *al-Gazzawi* of Gaza, etc. A certain parochialism perhaps? It is curious, though significant, and possibly denotes the more individualistic and settled way of life of the Palestinians that their names are rarely in the plural as is the case of the Jordanians across the river. Palestine, itself a source of civilization, was always settled and has had a continuity of historical development. The peasants as well as city people have always paid taxes. Because of its continued settlement and its religious significance, its population has always been more devotional. Piety among men or women, Christian or Muslim, is a highly extolled virtue. The Palestinians have a terrific loyalty to their heritage, religious and cultural, a hospitable nature that cherishes traditional values, love for the family and respect for its elders. And though some of them wish to shed their past, blaming it for much of their present situation, most do not wish this, nor could they even if they wished to, escape their past and its values.

In contrast to the Jordanians, the Palestinians, on the whole, were more sophisticated, urbane and closer to the twentieth century. Perhaps their land, a holy land always hosting pilgrims of all nationalities, religions and creeds, had something to do with that. Open to the sea, Palestine has always been close to other cultures and peoples. It has featured in the imagination of the West since the conversion to monotheism at the hands of Palestinian missionaries. It is thus that there were always foreigners, visitors and pilgrims at its shores. No doubt the presence of the Jews and the Palestinian-Jewish association in Palestine was then on a friendly level. Surely the inhabitants, Arabs or Jews, prospered or suffered with the turn of the times. And because of the small size of Palestine[8] and its continued settlement since the dawn of history, its inhabitants acquired settled traits, mores and habits of the village, town or

---

8. Palestine covers an area of 27,009 square kilometers or about 10,429 square miles.

city, their process of thinking is more systematic and cyclical and still reflects a settled agricultural rhythm of life and existence: a peaceful people, more attuned to compromise than to violence or bloodshed. In fact, vengeance among some Palestinian peasants was not taken against persons. Often the aggrieved party would resort to peeling the bark off an enemy's olive tree, thus killing it. The avenger would exclaim, *"qata't rizqoh"* [I severed his source of livelihood rather than taking his life.]

## Political Behavior

Outside the Arab world, the treatment of Palestinians is also unique. Wherever they go, people are suspicious of their intentions. When passing through airports, they are meticulously and thoroughly searched. If they reside in a Western country, they find themselves constantly under attack by the media, their neighbors and even sometimes their friends. They are constantly on the defensive, having to explain their politics, activities, even their very existence. The truth is so twisted, they themselves often find they cannot discern its proper direction.

An Israeli column intrudes on their camps in south Lebanon, while an Israeli squadron is pounding it from the air and an Israeli flotilla is bombarding it from the sea. Begin or Shamir or Netanyahu explains to the world that this death and destruction is punishment for the terroristic Palestinians who the night before succeeded in aiming a lone shell against an Israeli settlement. The world [i.e., the part of the world that counts] understands the Israeli action. The part of the world that produces and manufactures machines and weapons of war and destruction understands. Of course the Malians, the Sri Lankans or possibly the South Americans also understand the Palestinian reaction and despair. But surely we know that the understanding of a politician in London or Washington is deeper, more meaningful and weightier than that of others outside the Western world. Surely George Orwell was right: "Some animals are more equal than others." In fact, international aggression is portrayed as heroism: books, plays and films are written about it. Witness Entebbe.

Not only the Palestinians, but also the entire Arab world, whether leftist or rightist, progressive or reactionary, monarchist or republican, a close friend of the Western world or not, has utterly failed to explain itself to the world. Not only does no one seem to understand, no one seems to want to understand. It is not as if the Arabs are speaking an interstellar language hitherto undeciphered by humanity. No. The misunderstanding is deliberate.

And with the passage of time, further loss of self-esteem and self-confidence causes further erratic, often irrational, statements and actions. If the Palestinians wave the olive branch, as they have done since 1974, no one listens, for the Western world has been hypnotized by a propaganda machine that captured not only its imagination, but also seemingly its very heart.

No compromise with terrorists. Somehow this is understood by people who were once French freedom fighters, British or American liberators, and even Italian patriots. The double standard is baffling. And regardless of whether the

Palestinian or Arab leader is a "moderate" traditional friend or not, it seems impossible to get the point across, nor do the listeners comprehend. There is talk but there is no comprehension or communication. Is it because the other side has turned off the switch?

Often I wonder why the Arabs, Palestinians or non-Palestinians have persevered in these attempts for so long and why they still do. Why, for instance, do they not look for a solution elsewhere? Why do they not become truly terrorists? Why, in their desperation, do they not align themselves with the devil? I have, like most Palestinians or Arabs, rationalizations to explain this. Yet in my heart I know they are not reasons – not convincing ones anyway. Possibly because terrorism causes greater agony? Or is it because the price of terrorism is greater than what we would like to pay? Or is it because, ultimately, terrorism dehumanizes the terrorists as it does the terrorized? East or West, Palestinians, Jordanians, or the rest of the Arabs, find rationalizations, but not convincing reasons.

And it is thus that we continue to lie prostrate and helpless for the time being, hoping that the socio-economic development now taking place in the Arab world will, one day, lead to the wrong being righted. The realization is beginning to dawn that the job that has to be done cannot be done by proxy, by depending on someone else's manpower, resources, weapons, technology or brains. Ultimately justice will not be achieved without liberating the Arabs, Palestinians or Jordanians, from the fetters of ignorance and underdevelopment from which they suffer. Ultimately, we have to stand on our own feet and depend on our own resources.

The Intifada of the 1980s is just another phase of our struggle. We are beginning to understand that to live in the twentieth century means that we have to become familiar with its tools, methodologies, cruelties and ideas. That, we do know. And if now the Palestinians are made to feel like they are a rude intrusion on the civilized world, that feeling will pass when they become more familiar with the game and its rules – rules that change very quickly in response to Zionist needs and tactics.

## The State of Palestine

Palestine politics is as complicated as the problem, and as varied. This is partly because for a very long time Palestinians have been denied recognition. It is difficult for them to understand such a denial. Has their status deteriorated so much that they cannot set up a mini-state on what is left of Palestine: the West Bank and Gaza? No one asks whether Qatar, Kuwait, Gambia or Luxembourg are viable entities, so why are doubts cast concerning the viability of the hoped-for Palestinian state, when it is the Palestinians themselves who efficiently run much of the state machinery of many of the mini-states of the Arab world? Is every political entity, every state now in existence, the result of a rational, logical process of calculated thinking?

Of course a West Bank and Gaza state would be economically viable. For one thing, how many states in the world today, large of small, are completely economically viable? Also, it depends on what level of viability we are talking about, and this would depend to a large measure on the labor and the will of the Palestinian people themselves. In Arabic, we have a saying: 'Men make wealth' and not the other way round. The Palestinian people have shown themselves to be as tenacious and strong willed as any other group under stress. Their state, should that ever become a reality, would become the focal point of their pride and attention. For they are as dedicated to their ideals and rights as the Jews. It is certain that they will build a highly sophisticated and modern society, for, they will want it to peacefully compete with its neighbor, Israel. The Palestinians of the diaspora will undoubtedly contribute time, talent and resources to their homeland.

The viability of the Palestinian state will depend on the terms of its creation. If it is to be a peaceful region whose resources are not expended on military preparedness, this will certainly enhance the chances of its success. Under such circumstances, it is to the benefit of all the states in the region to have the addition of such an economically and politically stable state.[9] In the initial stages, compensation to the Palestinians for their property will be of great help.[10] Aid from international sources as well as bilateral foreign aid will have to play a major role. Aid from Arab countries will be forthcoming

---

9. Professor Walid Khalidi, a prominent Palestinian intellectual, went to great lengths to explain and emphasize the peaceful aspects of his visualized Palestinian state. See his article 'Thinking the Unthinkable: A Sovereign Palestinian State' in *Foreign Affairs*, July 1968.

10. Some Palestinian statesmen and intellectuals reject the idea of compensation. Rouhi al-Khatib, mayor of Jerusalem, in an interview in Amman, asked: "How can one accept compensation for his citizenship? Palestine is ours, not anybody else's."

and will be generous. That is not all. Ultimately, it is the people and their land that will have to produce viability.

The people are as dedicated to their national ideals as ever. Their pride in being Palestinian will serve as a constructive impetus to the rebuilding of their land. The land has never been a desert made to bloom by Jewish settlers. If it were thus, it would not have produced what it has already produced: civilizations, ideas, ideologies, personalities, prophets and religions. Ridden with strife for the past few decades, its orchards and valleys are wasted at present, but this would be righted in a peaceful situation.

The State of Palestine, with its geographic location at the heart of the area, can serve as a transit link, a *terra media*, a service center and certainly a tourist attraction. At one time, people questioned the economic viability of Jordan, as well as that of many other states. No one will deny the existence of difficulties, but the determined will of its people, a region and a world bent on peace can smooth out the difficulties.

And now that Jordan has, since 1988, severed all legal and administrative ties with the West Bank, and the Palestinian state has been declared, it is only logical for Israel, the United States, indeed the international community, to work toward a peaceful settlement. Both war and peace start in the hearts and minds of men and it is well for the Israelis, who suffered so much from the West, to remember that the chance for peace is now in their hands. Otherwise, only the radicals from both sides will be in the arena. If both continue to speak in millennial terms, which are almost identical, another war will result, perhaps another holocaust.

The radicals on the Arab side think that wherever Israel goes and whatever it does, it will always be surrounded by Arabs, and that even if there were a nuclear, biological or chemical war, or a combination of all three, there would still be enough Arabs at the end of it to inhabit the land. And while they recognize that this price would be high, they insist that is the only language that Israel and the West understand.

Logical? Who knows and who cares? The entire history of Palestine, indeed of the whole region, has never been logical, and the radicals point also to the lack of logic of the Israelis and their allies. Shamir, Sharon, Begin, Arens, Netanyahu, Bennett, do not speak the language of modern diplomacy or even war, but in millennial biblical terms only. They thunder down pronouncements harking back to ancient biblical prophets, Elijah, Amos and others. Shamir "smites" and the former Israeli Air Force chief, Ben Noon, behaved in the same way as his ancestor, Joshua Ben Noon, when he entered Jericho and leveled it.

The imagery and the symbolism are so strong: both sides are bewildered, though for different reasons, existing in a world where reality and illusion are intertwined. And the Israelis have been adept at creating new "realities" and new "facts" from ancient myths. The Palestinian, puzzled and bewildered at this terrible visitation, wonders what he has done to deserve what Israel, in anger and frenzy, is meting out to him. He did not do it, he cries, it was Hitler, it was in Germany, Poland, Russia, Hungary, France, even America, where the Jews suffered, were beaten and were discriminated against, and not in Palestine. "Why then am I paying the price?" he laments. He tries to understand what is happening not only to himself, but also to the Jew. He tries to understand and feel for the Begins, the Shamirs and others, escapees of Hitler's death camps, their skin tattooed, their souls seared and their hearts singed and burning. He tries to understand that these, and many other Israelis who suffered, cannot think straight, still suffering the mental and the physical agony of Western pogroms, death camps, social ostracism and discrimination. He tries and he makes excuses for himself and the Jew.

But the Palestinian has not been able to understand the depth of hatred and enmity meted out to him by Western politicians and statesmen. If Shamir lashes out in a frenzy of anger and wrath, breaking bones, cluster-bombing or napalming Palestinians, there may be some excuse: the man has never been accused of love, logic or mercy. He is, after all, still running from Hitler's demons who made lampshades out of the skin of his kin. He saw Hitler's doctors experimenting on Jewish children and women. The man is angry, frustrated, afraid, and even paranoid. But what is the matter with those world leaders who for the past 40 years have behaved as if nothing was being perpetrated against the Palestinians, indeed against the Arabs? Why the deep-seated hatred? Why do they continue to this day, six years after the Intifada and all the terrible ugliness that the Israelis commit, not to dare say the word to hold back the Israeli hordes and their wrath?

Why does the West still arm and support Israel without reservation? Why has the West, too, dehumanized the Palestinians and reduced them to objects? This puzzles the Palestinians. It puzzles them that the same people claiming to champion democracy and human rights deny them, in the same breath, the most elemental human rights. Even the animals in the West are better treated than the Israelis treat the Palestinians. Why the double standard and why the hatred?

# The Stories

# Mahmoud

Mahmoud smiles in puzzlement. He wants to know why I am asking him all these questions about himself, his family and about Palestine. From my accent he can tell I am an east Jordanian and that is enough to convince him I must be sent by the government. He is thinking very hard and fast. From the way he looks at me, I can detect his suspicion and sense the fear pouring into his veins. 'Are not most east Jordanians with the government anyway?' He must be thinking I am from the police, the secret police, otherwise why would such a well-dressed man bother to ask so many questions about him, a humble newspaper peddler on the street.

"No, I am not from the police." And I emphasize to him that I am a professor at the University of Jordan who is interested to know his life story for a small book I am writing on the Palestinians.

Looking at him, I can detect another feeling cross his face. Not fear, but caution mixed with a certain amount of skepticism. Indeed, he must be now thinking why would a professor from the university condescend to wish to know about his life, the story of his family and its roots.

"Please believe me, I am a professor at the university and I am very interested in your affairs, no, not your personal affairs, but I am interviewing several Palestinians on the subject of their life histories, their movements, fears, ambitions, anything that may give me a deeper insight into their life. Please forgive my intrusion into your personal life, but I do mean to explain to myself, to the world and maybe to you, what happened, indeed, what is happening."

A young boy is now very close, approaches, enthralled by our conversation. The boy looks at the newspaper peddler and says: "But Mahmoud, this man looks decent and what would you lose by telling him the story. Tell him, why are you afraid?"

Mahmoud is angry with the boy and he curses him profusely. I felt anger and pity: anger caused by his reaction to the young boy's intrusion and pity for seeing so much suspicion and fear in the heart of one man. I was also angry with myself for being so careless of the man's feelings and for intruding into his life so carelessly, ineptly. Why did I not find someone to introduce me to him? Before I departed, I left him a card with my address and telephone number.

Almost a month passed and I had forgotten the incident with Mahmoud completely when, one day, my secretary announced that a certain Mahmoud Sayyed wanted to see me. "Who is he?" I asked. She did not know, and I walked back with her to the reception area where I found Mahmoud with another younger and better-dressed man. Something had definitely changed in him. He looked not only apologetic but exceedingly shy. The younger man with him was, as it turned out, his brother, who had just graduated from the university. They told me that Said, the younger brother, recognized my name and had persuaded his older brother to come apologize and to talk to me.

Their story was a simple one. In fact, I have heard it from so many Palestinians that I do not know how much depth it may give to my portrait of them. Once I read that the sight of so much misery immunizes one against further sympathy, empathy or feeling. Is this so, and is this why I so callously question whether the repetition of disaster lessens its impact? Does the sufferer really worry whether the true story of the horror of his life has lost impact? Misery shares with death the ultimate realization that it is real.

* * *

Mahmoud, who was born in 1940, does not remember very much.

"I come from a village called Zir'een, one of the villages of the plain of Marj Ibn Amer that lies on the Palestine coast ..." In his mind, wish and fact merged so long ago he cannot distinguish between them. The myth is that Zir'een was a spot in heaven, where, had he and his family remained, nothing would go wrong, where life would have had a different and a nicer rhythm, perhaps, he grants that much. The fact is that Zir'een was a village on the beautiful plain of Marj Ibn Amer, the flat fertile plain of the eastern Mediterranean, a plain that bloomed in season with the fragrance of orange, lemon, tangerine and other citrus fruit blossom. The sight was magnificent, with the fruit ranging in color from deep green to bright orange when ripe, and his mother walking by his side. That is what Mahmoud remembers.

After the rains and in the spring, Mahmoud remembers the sandy earth beneath his bare feet. It felt refreshingly cool and clean. His father, a tall dark man with crossed, dark eyes, was a policeman in the government of Palestine. He remembers that he was proud of his father who, in turn, was proud of his uniform. He can still see his father walking the streets of Zir'een and can recall the respect people accorded him.

"Zir'een, my beautiful village, was demolished by the Israelis in 1950. They brought bulldozers and erased the entire village from the face of the earth. I have no idea what stands in its place now. No, I do not care to go back there and find out. I do not like to visit Palestine and I have not been back even to the West Bank, since 1967. I am not a political man and I do not want to be one. All I want is to be able to return to my home one day and to take my children and raise them where I was raised." Mahmoud was irritated by my questions and his younger brother was looking embarrassed.

"No," he said, "we were thrown out from Zir'een in 1948, two years before it was demolished. I remember the night we left. There was much shooting and screaming and my father led us out of the house to the orchards nearby. It was toward evening that he returned to the house by himself and brought back with him some blankets, food and my mother's *sigha* [gold jewelry]. My mother cried when he handed her the gold. She asked, though with resignation, 'Are we not going back?' My father did not answer. But we never went back and we do not know what happened to our furniture, pictures and household goods and utensils."

Mahmoud does not remember how they walked or got to the Jenin refugee camp. Nor does he remember their first few nights. He cannot recall where they slept or what they ate. He remembers the dirt floor of their tent and the very cold dark nights they spent in it. He cannot remember either how the tent turned into a tin, wood and corrugated iron room, with no bathroom or kitchen, and with the several of them huddled together in the evening to keep warm.

Eventually, his father got a job as a night-watchman for the camp's shopkeepers. How the camp sprouted so many shops selling food, second-hand clothing and shoes he cannot remember, yet he can remember his mother's tears when his father brought home his first pay. It was only five dinars but his father said: "It is better than nothing and anyway five dinars a month is five dinars a month, and that is something steady." His father, a proud man who had always lived by a strict code of honor and self-reliance, liked steady, sure things.

The rebuilding of their life was difficult. "How does one rebuild in the midst of chaos and uncertainty?" his father would ask. His mother would sigh, her eyes always misty now and reply: "Abu Mahmoud, be patient. God is good with us, at least we have some income and you are working. Wait, something will change." Mahmoud used to sit and listen.

"I always wondered about my mother's determination. At night when they thought that we children slept, they would talk, often until dawn. My mother would argue and argue but it seemed he had made up his mind. He wanted to emigrate to Brazil. 'But where is Brazil?' my mother would ask. He did not know, but he had some friends who had friends who had emigrated and they told him it was good and a place where a man could build a future. 'But maybe we will return,' my mother would say. 'Return, return? Ah! When will we return? Never. Look, it is already several years since the disaster, and we have not returned. All we hear is lies. No one wants us back in Palestine and no one is working toward it. Keep quiet woman, I have to go and build a new future. God willing within months I will send for you and the children.' Thus went the argument night after night. My father never tired of arguing with my mother. He wanted her convinced. He did not want just to leave, he wanted her blessing."

Eventually Um Mahmoud, Mahmoud's mother, gave him her gold bracelets, rings and other jewelry and in 1960 Mahmoud's father sailed from Beirut to Brazil.

"Oh yes, at first he wrote letters and sent us some money. In the beginning, he used to write once or twice a month and we used to wait for his letters hoping that in the next one he would ask us to join him. He never did. I do not know when he stopped writing altogether, it was several years later. Yet we know about him – you see we have some cousins in Brazil who tell us about him once in a while. We know that he is now married to a Brazilian called Anna and that they have one boy whom they call Zuhair. Zuhair is now fourteen years old and my cousins say he is a nice fellow. I would like to meet my brother one day.

"I think my father is ashamed. That is why he does not write to us but we know he asks about us from our cousins. We are ... I am not bitter about him nor is my mother. My mother ... she likes him and respects him very much. Sure, she was upset when she heard of his marriage but she is over it now and she hopes that one day we will see him again."

Addressing me, Mahmoud smiles and says, "Doctor, *el-hajjeh* [the pilgrim, meaning his mother] is a patient woman, she understands men."

Mahmoud told me that his father has a small grocery store in the capital, Brasilia, and owns a private car. He said that with some pride. Once in a while they send his father a message via the radio or via his cousins. Other than that they have no communication with him at all.

Mahmoud does not remember much about their village of Zir'een. All, or most, of his knowledge comes from his mother. She told him they had a small piece of land that was worked by his uncle, his father's elder brother, who planted it "with melons, cucumbers, sometimes sesame."

Mahmoud would look at his watch several times. It was obvious that he was getting impatient and wanted to go back to his work. "Yes, yes, my mother is still alive. Now she lives in Jabal al-Jawfeh" [one of Amman's lower middle-class residential areas]. "She lives with my unmarried brother Musa, and my brother Yusif and his wife and children. Yusif has a son, twelve years old, and a daughter, two months old. The house is not bad; it has two rooms, a bathroom and a kitchen. Of course, they have electricity and running water. No, they have no central heating. Yes, they have a butane gas stove and small new Italian refrigerator. All of them sleep on mattresses on the floor at night. Musa now has a job in the government and Yusif is the headmaster of a small government elementary school in al-Jawfeh district."

Mahmoud was proud of his and his family's accomplishments. "We lived *bi'araq jabeenah* [with the sweat of our brow] ... but we will build a better future for our children ... I hope better than what we had. ... I have my own apartment, but God willing, I will build a house for my mother and my family.

My wife, a cousin of mine, she would like my mother to live with us. We have two daughters three and two years old and already she is pregnant. I hope it is a boy. My wife thinks my mother would help her with the children. No, I cannot help. You see, I already have too many jobs. In the morning I teach at a government school in al-Quwaismah, a village near Amman. Then from noon till mid-afternoon I sell newspapers till my brother Musa takes over from me and in the evening I become a service taxi-driver. By the time I get home I like to play with my children, eat and rest. That is my life and my story, Doctor." He said that in such a way as to say, enough is enough, I have to go back to work now.

He left and I sat down and gazed at the wall. I forgot to ask him several things. For instance, how did they live after his father's departure? How did he and his brother acquire enough education to become teachers? They must have finished high school at least. When did they move to Amman? How? Why? I decided to look him up again. Weeks later when I sat down to look again at what I had recorded, I decided it was better to leave the questions unanswered.

Once in a while, I pass the street where he sells his papers, and from afar, I look at him and wonder about his determination.

Originally an emergency camp established to accommodate Palestine refugees fleeing the 1967 Arab-Israeli war, this youngster in Baqa'a emergency camp, Jordan, became a permanent refugee in exile.

© 1968 UNRWA Archive Photo by Odd Uhrbom

Wadi Dleil refugee camp was one of the first emergency tented camps set up on the east Jordan plateau following the hostilities in June 1967. It was closed at the start of winter and the refugees moved to new camps in the east Jordan Valley where the winter climate is milder.

© 1967 UNRWA Archive Photo by George Nehmeh

# Odeh

Adil, the son of Odeh, never saw his home-town of Abu Qash near Jerusalem in Palestine, now called the Occupied Territories and Israel. At his wake, his father stated this fact as if it were more terrible than his son's death.

"Yes," Odeh said, "we still have some land in Abu Qash that my relatives now cultivate, but I have no desire to go back and visit my birthplace, never. I went once in 1972 and I do not wish to repeat the humiliating treatment I received from them [the Israelis] at the bridge. The indignity of the search, the long hours of waiting in terror before they let you in, the insults. I will never see Palestine again, but I know that my progeny will see it and will repossess it; maybe a hundred years into the future, and maybe more, but they will repossess it."

In his bitterness and anger Odeh seemed to have forgotten about the death of his son. His recent experience with his son's death appeared to have deepened his desperation.

"Adil," he told me, "died only last night after spending five months in a coma at the local hospital."

"How did he die?" I asked, and Odeh looked more than thoughtful, a cloud hovering somewhere behind his eyes. He did not seem to want to answer, but then decided he would and what he said surprised and saddened me.

"Doctor, now I have only two sons and four daughters. With Adil I had three sons." He said that as if to make sure of his arithmetic, and then he added: "The saddest thing is that his death is such a waste. He did not die a martyr or even with any meaning. As a draftee in the Jordanian Army he was riding in an army truck when the driver had to stop suddenly and he hit the back of his head on an iron bar in the truck. No blood. He looked as if asleep for five months and yesterday he died. God gave and God took, what can I do? And now hope is dead with him. *El-hajjeh* [the pilgrim, referring to his grandmother] is heartbroken and I am heartbroken for her. You see, she just arrived from Abu Qash with two of my uncles, too late for the funeral."

He looked away as a young boy brought a long spouted kettle full of water and started to sprinkle the dusty floor of the goat-hair tent that Odeh had set up across the street from his modest cement-block house to receive the condolences of his friends and relatives. Across the street, the door to his house was open and several women in Palestinian and Jordanian peasant clothes, their heads covered in white shawls, were crying silently. Once in a while a loud wail was heard. Another young man brought the pot of *qahweh sadah*, bitter Arab coffee made with cardamom seeds, and started filling small handleless cups to pass around to the group. A group of new mourners was arriving and Odeh and his elder and younger brothers got up to receive them. The whole scene was traditional, almost biblical; the goat-hair tent with its dusty floor, the low chairs and cushions and the women dressed as women had always dressed in this part of the world.

A discussion was going on about the latest Gulf crisis and one young man declared with some conviction that Saddam

Hussein was not truly defeated. "Is it a defeat when the whole world gangs up on you, including your supposed Arab and Muslim brothers?" he asked. No one bothered to answer him. In fact, the man seated next to him looked at him as if he had just arrived from outer space and as if wondering what kind of a question that was.

"What of Abu Qash?" someone asked one of the two uncles who had arrived late for the funeral. "What about it?" he replied, and then he added as an afterthought: "We survive, we live, they are strong and merciless, but we fight back. It is not an easy life. In fact, it may not be life at all, but we stay and we hold on to our land and memories. Life is never easy with the Israelis. You can never gauge their mood and you can never tell what they might do next. Worse still, you can never tell the truth from lies with them – each says something different from the other. Whom do you believe? Sharon? Levy? Shamir? Peres? Whom?"

Odeh, in the meantime, was listening and he looked somewhat disgusted. Adil's death seemed to have been especially devastating for him. It was, as he put it, "so unnecessarily wasteful."

One of the uncles said: "He [Odeh] had called my older brother that morning around seven o'clock to report his son's death and to see if we knew anybody at the Red Cross headquarters in Amman to relay the message to his relatives in Abu Qash. My brother called me and I tried to get in touch with the Jordan radio station, which ordinarily passes messages and information from Palestinians to each other not only 'across the bridge' in the Occupied Territories and Israel but throughout the world. They were very cooperative. They would report the death at the end of the 10 o'clock morning news, but that would be too late for Odeh's relatives to make arrangements with the Israeli authorities to come to Amman in time for Adil's funeral at one o'clock. Finally, my brother got the Red Cross to fax the message and the relatives arrived. The anxiety, however, remained.

"One of the officials at the radio station said that Kawther would be happy to relate the message. 'Miss Kawther al-Nashashibi broadcasts messages for Palestinians throughout the world. Her 12 o'clock program, also repeated an later hour, is anxiously awaited by Palestinians the world over. Why don't you use it?' I explained this would be too late for the funeral."

The incident reminded me of Kawther's voice on Amman radio passing along messages: "Mahmoud so and so from the Bak'a refugee camp sends his greetings to all his relatives in the Gaza Strip. All is well with me and our family. My son, Ahmad, got married and my daughter Azizeh gave birth to a baby boy. We called him Mustafah. Anyone who is listening please tell my brother Yusif to arrange for a permit for me from the Israeli authorities to visit you sometime in the next few months. I received a letter from my brother Talal in Germany and he says that he and our other brother, Jala, in Brazil, are in good health and send their respects and greetings. All is well with us and soon I will be sending you twenty dinars via the Cairo-Amman Bank."

As I was musing over this and similar messages, new mourners arrived and Odeh and his brothers again sprang up to greet them. The afternoon sun was hot, drying the recently sprinkled water on the dusty floor of the tent and the rented wooden chairs were becoming uncomfortable. "God have mercy on his soul," we said. The man next to me said: "Nothing will remain except He who is Permanent."

As I left, I recalled Yitzhak Shamir's insistence on Jerusalem being the 'eternal' capital of Israel and Odeh's answer to our condolences, said with resignation as well as resolve: "Nothing is permanent except the face of God."

My mother's often-repeated remark, "His name freezes on the water," came to my mind.

Jerusalem is a holy place for Jews Christian and Moslems.

# Sami

The smile on his face was shy, almost tentative, as if trying to hide a particular emotion from the world. I had met Sami only an hour before when he said to me in the very familiar Arab way, "Kamel, I already sense that I like you, and that we can be friends." The simple statement shocked me as I was thinking that it was I who should be saying this, or something similar, to him. The situation was more awkward since at that moment we were sitting with a few other friends and acquaintances.

Later in the evening, when we were alone, he allowed me a few glimpses into his life. To him, nothing was unusual about it. He was neither proud nor apologetic, and when he began to open up in response to my questions, it was as if he was talking about someone else's life. I wondered at the detached voice in which he spoke.

"Only three tragedies have happened in my life and as I look back on them, Kamel, I cannot tell which one has affected me more than the other. I think often about them and I really cannot decide." At that moment his hand reached out but missed the cup of Arabic coffee he was drinking. He finally found it and took a sip, then replaced the cup carefully on the table where his hand could easily reach it.

"The first tragedy, which I now think is the least of my concerns, was when, at the age of four or five, I began to lose my eyesight. Slowly the light began to dim and with it the sound of joy in my mother's voice. My father tried desperately to halt the advancing disaster and though he had little money, he spared no expense. He took me to the best Arab and Jewish doctors in Palestine of those days. Then it was still called Palestine and Arabs and Jews were citizens of the same land, and to this day I harbor no hatred or ill feeling towards them. Even at the Jerusalem Hadasah Hospital they could do nothing. It was something congenital, they said, and nothing could be done. Sometimes I think that the Palestine problem and our Arab-Israeli conflict are congenital too. It seems to have taken the light away from the heart of both Arab and Jew. Only blind rage remains: a rage that is eating us from the inside out.

"By 1948, when I was eight years old, the second tragedy of my life occurred. By that time I was totally blind and, no, I did not even see any shadows at all. I did not see, but felt the loss of our land, the homeland of our nation and the lands around our village. You see, the armistice line cut exactly at the edge of our village, leaving it on one side and the lands we once tilled on the other. The first few years after the disaster of 1948 were the hardest for my mother and father. And though a child, my older brother used to sit and describe to me how my mother was slowly withering away. It ate at her heart to see our land being tilled by strangers and though only the barbed wire separated land from village, our land, she would cry, was further away than the moon.

"She would watch, wringing her hands, while our only milking cow was being milked by strangers wearing strange clothes. In church, with all her children around her, she would drop to her knees making promises before the Blessed Mary. Sometimes my father would laugh and say: 'You cannot bribe her you know. The Virgin will do only God's will, we must endure.' One morning, my father woke up and found her dead by his side. Till the day he died he never shed a tear and I was told by my older brother he never looked at another woman again.

"A week after the death of my mother, he took me to the government school for the blind where they taught rattan work, weaving and some other useful skills. El-Mudeer, [the principal of the school] after giving me some tests, reprimanded my father: 'This is a very intelligent boy. What do you mean bringing him here to me? What are you trying to do? Bury him? Take him away and send him to some regular school to learn proper academic subjects. He is brilliant.' And so it was that my father sent me to a regular school where I did very well, eventually graduating from high school with top honors. And through our church in the village and with the help of some friends, I was given a scholarship to the American University of Beirut.

"Beirut was then tranquil, a center of culture, arts and ideas, and I enjoyed every minute of it. Those were some of the happiest days of my life." There was a ring to his voice when he said this. "You see, Doctor, I always had a way with girls. And I played on my blindness unashamedly and thus never lacked for female companionship. They, too, knew I was just playful and thus enjoyed my carefree company without any promises or hopes. Those were beautiful days. The girls would come to my room or we would go to the Mediterranean Sea shore on the edge of the campus and they would read me my books. And while I learned, they learned too and often in the summer evenings we would discuss poetry or philosophy or history well into the night.

"We always came back to the subject of Palestine and how one day our land would be returned. It used to strike me as funny in those days that even Lebanese or Tunisian girls would talk about Palestine as 'our land'; now I understand better. I do not know why but I feel better. It is as if the whole Arab world becomes Palestinian once in a while when someone talks or reminisces about Palestine. You know, by the way, Doctor, that I wrote a book about the Palestinians, don't you?

"And so the second tragedy of my life was the loss of Palestine; a land that I was once privileged to see when a child and now no more. It gives the loss a deeper meaning that I literally cannot see it now, in addition to the fact that it has become the home of someone else.

"The third tragedy of my life was when my wife decided to divorce me. That's it. Now you know the whole story of my life."

I thought to myself that that was not true. I must have some details. How did he go to America? Where did he study? When did he get married? To whom? Why did she divorce him? Does he have any children? There were too many questions running through my mind and I needed some answers.

That same evening, after having finished dinner at the restaurant of the Marriott Hotel in Amman, I tried to get Sami to continue.

"I am tired," he said. "The memory of the divorce is too recent and too painful still."

Not until two days later was I able to get him to open up again.

"What can I tell you about my life now? It feels empty and I feel there is a heavy weight on my chest while a cold hand squeezes my heart.

"I knew my wife from the first week I reached America. Studying in Washington was a pleasure and her friendship at first, and then later her love, made it more of a pleasure for me. Like me, she loved Washington and she used to sit and describe it to me by the hour. In turn, I would tell her about my village near Jerusalem, its little church, my family and making up most of the village inhabitants. She never believed we had snow in winter or that we sang Christmas carols, carrying candles in our hands, at Kaneesat al-Mahdi, the Church of the Nativity in Bethlehem.

"When I got my Ph.D. we got married and to this day I think it was the happiest day of my life. From then on, my life was like a dream, a succession of happy events, until the day I returned from a one-week trip to Germany.

"After marriage, I secured a teaching position in the Midwest. Life was smooth and soon I knew everyone in town and everyone knew me. What made and continues to make my life more pleasant is the computer that I now have. I do not need people to read for me anymore; it can read to me out loud and when I become bored with one voice I can switch to another. It has sixteen different voices to choose from and it has opened up all the libraries of the world for me and it can store and retrieve information. I never knew there was so much knowledge in the world and now that I have this computer I keep discovering how ignorant I really am.

"Between marriage and divorce twelve years passed, which I spent in complete happiness and contentment. Anna used to complain when I came home a few minutes late and we developed the habit of sitting with our two daughters, now 8 and 4 years old, and talking for an hour after dinner and before the girls went to bed. We talked about my work, my salary, planned vacations, visiting my older brother and his family in the small town close by, anything. The favorite subject for my wife Anna, however, and eventually for our two little daughters was about my life in the old country. Especially the little ones – they wanted to know about their grandmother and our simple village life in Palestine. To this day, I cannot explain to them, nor could I really successfully explain to Anna, how we lost Palestine. Sometimes she would get angry at me, as if I alone was responsible. That we were backward simple folk, who were no match for the intelligence and meticulous planning of a world Zionist organization, was no explanation for her. Something else had to be wrong, she would insist. 'Instead of blaming the British and now the Americans, you should blame only yourselves.'

"On and on our discussions would go, and once in a while, after the children went to bed, she would offer me an apology. Nevertheless, I was happy and in fact I never seriously thought I would go back to Palestine even if the chance presented itself. What would I do there, Doctor, a blind man like me. In any case with my lectures, books and articles I am more of a help to my people in America than anywhere else.

"It is the third tragedy that made the previous two manifestations pale in comparison. I have learned to live with the loss of Palestine and my sight, but I do not know if I can live with the loss of Anna. Even the way it happened is unbelievable. Until she said goodbye to me at the airport, crying at my departure and asking me to hurry home, everything was as it had always been. When I returned from the week's seminar in Germany, where I read a paper on the Arab-Israeli conflict, Anna was not the Anna I knew. In the house there was a different person that I had never known.

"I knew something was wrong when she did not meet me at the airport as she said she would. Telephone calls to the house went unanswered and fearing the worst, I finally took a taxi home. She was not at home when I arrived and I felt the house uncharacteristically messy, with unpleasant smells coming from the kitchen. Anna was always very neat and orderly. She kept everything in place for my sake too. She knew that it would help me and she was faithfully tidy always. And though a little while later she arrived with our daughters, it felt like a long time had passed. The little one was crying and Anna never even said hello. Instead she said, 'Sami, I am a liberated woman now and I want a divorce. While you were away I moved out of the house and got myself an apartment. I only came back to return your daughters to you and am now leaving.' To my questions as to what had happened, what was going on and why, I received no reply. Instead, I heard the door slam and she was gone. Oh yes, I tried to talk with her and I even got our friends and my brother to intervene on my behalf, but to no avail. More than the fact that I miss her, it breaks my heart to hear the little one crying even now, one year later, 'where is my mommy?' No, I do not know what happened in my absence but you know many women in America have been doing the same thing in the last few years. She is now living with a man of unsavory character, and I still do not know why. Of course, I would take her back any time – if not for me, then for our two daughters. No, the older one never asks about her mother. I think she feels betrayed and now she is developing a very strong attachment to the woman who takes care of them and cleans the house."

I was more stunned when he said, after a few moments of silence, "You know, Kamel, since she left I keep bumping into every object around the house, as if further blindness has been added to my earlier one. I do not know for whom I should feel more sorry; myself, my little one and her sister or our people in Palestine."

Palestine refugees initially displaced to Beach Camp in Gaza board
boats in search of a better life in Lebanon or Egypt.

Palestine refugee boys pose for the camera, behind them lies Beach camp,
where they and their families live, Gaza.

© 1970 UNRWA Archive Photographer Unknown

# Tuhfeh

Husam was born in 1967, a few months before the June 5 War when Israel attacked and took from Palestine what it did not occupy in 1948: the West Bank, the Gaza Strip [between 1948 and 1967 under Egyptian administration], and the Syrian Golan Heights. Husam, Tuhfeh's grandson, does not recall the events; any recollection comes through his father, "who talks a lot about it and about the 1948 events too".

Originally the family came from Jaffa, on the east coast of the Mediterranean, which his father tells him was very beautiful: "*Aroosa* [a virgin bride]. It is sad I, too, cannot live those days of prosperity and glory." The memory, handed down from father to son, from grandmothers and aunts, seems to enhance the romance and the beauty of the ancient seaport city. The passage of time, like the mist that at times engulfs the city, only exalts its image in the mind. And the selective collective memory of aunts and uncles pushes away all that may have been unpleasant. Grandchildren of the children of Jaffa, *Yafa* in Arabic, to this day exclaim *ya waladi alaiki ya Yafa,* an untranslatable slang that expresses the desolation and sadness a man from Jaffa feels when the memory of the city strikes.

Husam, a child of 1967, now in his third home, in Amman, does not remember the first home or, indeed, the second, in Nablus. And yet, his knowledge of Jaffa is intimate, all with a texture of its own: the sand, the water and the wall nearby from which his ancestors used to jump into the sea to swim, his father had told him.

Al-Sahayneh [the Zionists] have surely spoiled it, his father had told him. "Everything they touch they desecrate and sadden." Husam said: "I love Amman, even the narrow dusty street on which I grew up near al-Nasr refugee camp, but I also yearn for Palestine, all of it and Yafa in particular. I wonder if the Zionists will ever permit me to see it. As a driver, I know the distance is not very much, but when I look at the map, Germany seems closer. How did the memory of Palestine survive? But then, how too, did it survive in the hearts of the Jews for so long?"

The collective memory, product of the oral history passed on from generation to generation, is as strong as a stake deep in the ground and it ties Husam, like it does his father, to Palestine. "The roots are too deep, what can I do?" he says.

His grandfather died of the "bad disease", cancer, he thinks, and then he hastily adds: "People did not know in those days, there was no consciousness of these things." He says this in such a way as to give the feeling that had they had "consciousness", they could have prevented the disease, or at least cured it. "It is a pity, isn't it?" he adds.

He died, Husam was told, at the age of 30, leaving behind his wife Tuhfeh, which means *objet d'art*. Husam's father was then 10 or 11 years old, and the eldest of a family with three daughters. How did Tuhfeh, his grandmother, survive – a refugee from camp to camp, with no money, no legacy or resources?

"But then you should understand, Professor, that my grandmother Tuhfeh was truly a Tuhfeh. A precious jewel she was.

God rest her soul, she died two years ago, and I remember her well. She always embroidered her own *fellah thobe* (peasant costume), always with the needlework and the stitch of Yafa. You could tell she was from Yafa the minute you saw her in her *thobe* and the white shawl covering her head. To the last day of her life she worked at the UNRWA clinic, first scrubbing floors. Later, she had a better job as an assistant cook. We always had plenty to eat." And then Husam's mood changed. "Poor woman, her palms felt like wood, hard with cracks and her face was full of wrinkles. But I loved her, and used to wait for her when she came home in the evening. I would sit on her lap and she would tell me what she had done that day and of the old, old days that had passed: of Nablus, Yafa and Palestine.

"She would be tired and almost always smelling of *maqloobeh* [a kind of stew made with rice, sliced fried eggplant or cauliflower and chunks of lamb]. I used to love to listen to her old tales. She was never taught, she never went to school and yet, Doctor, she was smart and she knew about everything and had been many places and seen many things. She would say, 'God's mercy is wide and He took care of me so that I could take care of my children. I never had time to think I was a widow. You see, my son, God sometimes causes the death of a camel so that a fox can eat. And what good is a fox? But God has a wisdom that we sometimes cannot understand. Never forget that, and never question his judgment. You must accept. He knows, He knows.' Once she went to al-Quds, Holy Jerusalem, to visit the mosque. It is there that she saw the Hanging Rock, hanging in the air with nothing to support it. In the old days, before they built walls around it to make it look as if the rock is resting on them, the visiting pregnant women used to abort their babies from fright at witnessing such a sight. Since the wall, it does not happen any more. Maybe it is better they built it. I have never been to Jerusalem, although I would like to see the Aqsa and the Dome of the Rock mosques. My father too says they are magnificent. I wonder. Why cannot they, the Zionists, allow us to have peace with them? We no longer wish to fight, but then what is the matter with us? What is the matter with our leaders and why do they allow the situation to remain as it is? Is it hopeless, Doctor?

"The beautiful old days will never return, my father says. 'When a day is gone, it is gone and as the saying goes: that which goes, goes.' My father's grandfather was a fisherman and also he had a horse-drawn cab, which he worked in the evenings. They had boats and oranges as big as watermelons. And when he died, I do not know when – he had only one son, whose mother would not allow him to be a fisherman. The sea, they say, can sometimes be too dangerous and his mother was afraid for him. I saw the sea only once in Aqaba and I must say it did not look too dangerous. But then, I cannot swim. Anyway, his mother had some relatives where she sent him to learn to become a butcher. He married my grandmother, Tuhfeh, when they were very young, like they used to in the old days.

"By the way, I almost got married in 1989 when we started to have economic trouble in the country and the value of the dinar fell. It is a good thing I did not, though I would like to; but how can I manage? I can hardly manage as it is. I do have to help my father a little bit. He is getting old. He is nearly 58 and he should retire. I told him that I did not need to get married and that my salary would be enough to sustain the family, but he refuses. He says he likes to work although sometimes he comes home very, very tired. He is also sick. He developed a skin disease, psoriasis, which causes him a lot of pain. He says he developed it from a great fright when he had to hide with one of his cousins under a bridge, and eat wild *khurfaish* [an artichoke-like plant] for many days while the Zionists were passing overhead. I do not know when that was, but my father suffers from it since then. In any case, people tell me it is better that he continues to work. Idleness, they say, would kill him. The old man, you see, has too many memories to think about. I guess it is better that he works. Maybe that way his disease will go away, God willing.

"My grandfather, I am told, was the best butcher in Yafa. He had a generous and giving spirit; when he cut the meat he did not wish it for himself but hoped that his customer would enjoy it. And though he died young, he had *barakeh* (blessing). He also had barakeh to set people's broken bones and he did that. It is his *barakeh*, my grandmother said, that gave her strength and though, when young, she was beautiful and coveted by many men who wanted to marry her, she said she could never marry again and spoil his *barakeh*. Besides, with another husband, 'God forbid,' she would say, 'how could I properly raise your father and your three aunts?'

"My grandfather died in 1947 or 1948, I am not sure which, and then within a short time my grandmother and most of the Arabs of Yafa were driven out by the Zionists. My grandfather was buried in Yafa, God have mercy upon him. There was much shooting and looting. The Arab women were not safe from the Zionists and you know how we Arabs care so much for our female honor, and so my grandmother took my father, then 10 or 11 years old, and my three aunts and walked out. I do not know where the camp was. My grandmother refused to talk much about those days, but I will ask my father for you. They had a tent, some blankets and whatever rations the *Wakaleh* (UNRWA) gave them. Since then my father says he hates white *fasouliah* (white beans) and we never have it in our house. One day I would like to try it.

"I don't know how long my grandmother remained in the camp, but then, with my father, they moved us to Nablus, where my father worked as a waiter. God gave him, and soon he rented a small store, and opened a restaurant for day workers and the poorer class, and which he told me he called *al-Awdeh* (Return). God gave him again and he made some money. And then the 1967 war occurred and he left with those who left, and once again my grandmother and her family became refugees. My God, twice in a lifetime. They took the bus and came to Amman. Again they were given a tent, some blankets, and monthly rations from the *Wakaleh*. My father does not know why we left Nablus, but he says he was very frightened that maybe God, who saved them from the Zionist in 1948, would not spare them again. I was born in Nablus but I also love Amman. I still remember, though vaguely, our life in Mukhayam al-Nasr [the Nasr refugee camp] near the train station, east of Amman.

"My father could not find work and we had a very hard time. It was very cold in the winter, especially when we had snow, and very dusty and hot in the summer, and the food was always the same. And then, with God's help, my grandmother found work in the *Wakaleh* clinic. She worked there till the day she died. She tired herself for us, very much.

"She saved money at the clinic and from her savings, and from money from my aunts when they went to work, she built her family a house of cement. God bless her and rest her soul, she shielded the family. Soon she added separate apartments for each one of her daughters as each married. She had separate deeds made for each of the apartments in my father's and in each of my aunt's names. Now only one of them still lives there with her family. The other two rent out their apartments. No, my father does not mind. It was, after all, with the help of my aunts that my grandmother was able to do all of these things. She could not read or write, but she understood the value of education and had her three daughters trained as practical nurses. They were not very educated, but the youngest, my grandmother would not send to train until after she had finished high school. With the money she collected from my aunts, her own, and also my father's, who eventually found a job as an office boy in the neighborhood government school, she built the house and furnished each of the apartments. Of course after this, all my aunts got married. Now they have children, even grandchildren. One, as I said, still lives in the house, the second moved with her husband to a rented house in Jabal al-Hussein near his work and my third aunt, the eldest, moved a few years ago to America with her entire family. They have opened a grocery store in a city called Los Angeles and God opened his blessings on them. They are doing very, very well.

"They do not send any money to my father. My aunt in America used to send money to my grandmother regularly when she was alive. Now they send some presents and some money on big occasions: thank God we do not need it. I work as a driver for a local company and my father works, and, thank God, we have enough, although one of these days I would like to marry. Maybe when my younger brothers grow up. But even then how can I, with the responsibility of having to take care of my mother and father later on?

"When he was young, my father told me he used to steal dough and use it as fish bait. He can recall every street in Yafa although he says someone told him that the Zionists have changed its entire character. Even the street names have changed to Hebrew ones, and Yafa is now called Yafo. He was also told that the Jews have destroyed many mosques and houses and that once when they blew up a house with the people still in it, you could see, for days afterwards, human flesh stuck on the ruined walls. On that occasion, days later, they found a baby girl still alive as her crib had overturned and protected her from the falling rubble. God gave her a new life.

"Sometimes when my father talks I cannot tell what is fact and what is fiction. Both seem to have blended in his mind to create a new reality for him. The pain is certainly real and he says that from the moment he opened his eyes he felt little else but pain. My father still thinks that we will return. Sometimes I am not so sure, although I would like to. And of course my children will want to. He … we, live one day at a time although now with his old age my father thinks that the pain is less.

"It is my mother who laughs at these notions. With much bitterness she says to him: 'Abu-Husam, you have to abandon these notions, you are teaching your children to daydream just as you do.' And it is true, for I frequently find him sleeping with his eyes open, not caring about those around.

"Too many broken and false hopes did this to him. He does not live for the future but in the past. Imagine how much worse his situation would have been had he been older and more aware when he left Yafa. My God, he was only 10 or 11, and yet he is full of memories. I think it is the bitterness that is eating him and if he continues like this, he too might develop the bad disease just like his father.

"My mother would say, 'the difference is that I am from Nablus, Jabal al-Nar, the fire mountain as its people sometimes call it. We make soap there and we have to be alert and practical at all times, otherwise the ingredients would burn'."

Husam shook his head and added: "I always say that it is people that make life easy or difficult for themselves. 'If destiny wishes it so, then it must be so, and nothing can change it. That is written, and one has to be practical. Although we are transient in this life, we have a duty to do what we can for ourselves,' my mother would say. Sometimes I think my father is simply obstinate. What does he mean, we must fight forever for Palestine? Who will fight? Those in splendid villas in the rich neighborhoods of Amman, or the Palestinians scattered all around the world? I have a cousin in Australia, and another in Brazil. They must have other ideas by now. Also, the Arab governments have no desire, nor the will, nor even the means, to fight. Surely the Zionists were clever when they scattered us thus. How will all these Palestinians gather again, you tell me, who will fight? Sometimes I think our fight is more bitter against each other, but then, as my father says, what do I know? My conscious eyes were never graced with the sight of Palestine. It is like that; I think my father is right. Who cares whether or not he is practical? Who cares if the Zionists have dehumanized us? Someone told me that some of them think we are cockroaches. But as my father says, there are more of us, and even if there is a nuclear war, we would outlive them. Slowly, as you see, they are draining us of human feelings as they have drained themselves. I also think my grandmother would be very pleased if I agreed with my father. Until God changes things, Jabal al-Nasr [Victory Mountain], where we live will be our home."

Twice daily, once in the morning and later in the evening, the women
of Beach camp fill the largest containers they can carry with clean water
at a communal water point in Beach camp, the Gaza Strip.

A mother and her children stand next to a communal water point in
Khan Younis camp, Gaza Strip.

# Salem

Salem, the once proud fisherman, is sitting near his house, facing the blue Mediterranean. What does it matter if he lives in Acre or Askalan? His home, he knows, is Palestine and that is enough. The quiet of the afternoon is disrupted by an Israeli patrol helicopter flying overhead and by the Israeli radio announcer reading the news. He thought he had stopped listening a long time ago, 10, 15 or perhaps it was 20 years ago. But something seems to always draw him to listen in spite of himself; maybe in rebellion against the incessant and constant barrage of vilification his people are subjected to. Salem wonders if a free man can ever become a slave. Perhaps his body can, but certainly not his heart. He knows that is the reason the spirit of freedom never dies: for only the minds of few, very few men can really be completely fettered. Otherwise, how would the children know how it was? He knows he must endure these heavy shadows that blacken his soul and he recalls the proverb he once heard his mother tell his father: "Kiss the hand you cannot beat and wish that it be servered" That was in the days of the British. He wondered if his grandmother had said it in Ottoman times, too. She must have, for, he recalls that though she looked like a sweet, unsophisticated and simple peasant lady, she was always free spirited and forward looking.

The heat of the afternoon is truly oppressive. It is only the beginning of July, yet it feels like mid-August. Salem loosens the buttons of his shirt and his movement causes him to smell his odor. Not pleasant, he thinks, and his clothes are certainly dirty, yet what can he do? Today he bought shoes for Ahmad, nice brown shoes, and a smile crosses his face. Poor Ahmad was so happy with the new shoes. Surely they would have looked better had he had the money to buy him socks, but Ahmad did not seem to mind. "I hope they will last until Ramadan," he says, although he knows they will not.

It is Friday. That is why he did not even look for work today. Or is it because he was tired of scratching for a living; or because he wanted to stay with Amneh, his wife? "What is left of Amneh," he thinks. Twelve years ago, when they married, she was a beautiful girl with a lovely smile and deep dark eyes. Could the color of her eyes have faded too like their drab fearsome life? He cannot think any more. In fact he realizes he has not been thinking for months, even years. "What happened to his life? Her life? His people's life?" he wonders as the afternoon drags on and on.

An Israeli jeep with laughing soldiers passes, raising a cloud of dust. The fresh-looking soldiers were talking loudly and laughing. Salem looks like he feels sorrow for them. Or is it envy? Fear? Or hate? He could not tell, for he seemed to have said goodbye to laughter, security, peace of mind and happiness long ago. He has been married a long, long time. Twelve years ago he married Amneh. Her father, his uncle, said to him then: "Take good care of Amneh, she is so thin." Yes, she was like a bamboo reed. He recalls his wedding night. The wedding party was beautiful, with men from his clan, the tribe from Bir al-Sabi (Beer Sheba) dancing, brandishing their bamboo sticks and singing desert songs.

Another Israeli patrol jeep passes, raising more dust, He is beginning to sweat. Someone is talking inside his hut. It must be Amneh talking to Handal, their daughter. He thinks of Handal with a deep sense of sorrow. How will she survive, and who will marry her the way she limps? Though only 11, having arrived just ten months into their marriage, her legs have grown grotesquely fat. The doctor called it a disease whose name he could never remember, and prescribed medicine that never seemed to do any good, maybe because it was free from the UNRWA dispensary? Nothing seems to help, and bitterness fills his heart. Where is justice? The poor child is only 11 and already she is condemned without a hearing or trial. She passes by and he calls after her: "Where are you going, girl?"

She does not seem to hear and she does not answer, but continues to limp along up the dusty street. "God," he says, "with her limp and her huge legs she looks like a strange animal waddling along up and down. God, please help her, for I cannot." His eyes sting with his quiet tears and his helplessness. "What can I do, I, a poor day-laborer?"

Quiet settles on his mind and on the street and he feels his spirit drift away, far, far away to his birthplace, to his mother. He cannot seem to remember his father, who was killed when he was still small, and he never understood how, although he always meant to ask his mother, God rest her soul. It had something to do with a man called al-Qassam in the 1930s or 40s, he could not tell. He knows that other men of his family and his town, who knew his father, spoke of him with respect and even some love. There is no picture of him. His mother said that his father never took a picture of himself nor allowed one to be taken of him. She did not know whether it was for security reasons or because his father thought it was a sin, a shame. Salem would have liked to have a picture of his father to show Ahmad, his grandson.

His birthplace? The barren looking hills that wonderfully and miraculously turn green after the rain? How could he think of the spring in the winter of his own life, he thinks, and he smiles to himself. He must think of the goats and the sheep that grazed there, and of his flute, which he has "not thought about for years." The sheep, he says, would be quiet and settle down to its sound, while the goats never seemed to care. And in the evening, after he watered the animals from the well and chatted with the other shepherds, he would go home to his mother. He remembers how good the warm milk always tasted with the freshly baked flat, thin bread, and the pungent smell of the dung fire mixed with the aroma of sweet tea. Those were days of innocence and security that now seem will never be part of his life, but of someone else's. Amneh's tattered clothes and cracked feet wound him. "What happened to my pride?"

Where are the other members of his family, his clan? When they were forced to leave their territory, he refused to cross the border with them into Jordan. At that time, he thought death would be better. Was he right, and is he now alive? He cannot tell. Vaguely he knows they seem to have survived. A friend of his told him that he heard so on the radio. He heard someone from his family, now living in al-Bak'a refugee camp near Amman, sending him greetings, and informing him that they were well. He would hate to be called a refugee or *nazeh* [person displaced after 1967]. He hates the word, for it denotes not only rootlessness but also despair, hopelessness and helplessness. It is true that he is poor and did not work today, but he is not a refugee and he is still on his land – well, not exactly his land but at least his country.

Since he heard news of his relatives via the radio, he carries one with him at all times. It is small and he keeps it in his breast pocket lest it be bumped into by someone and broken. Whenever it is time, he turns it on and listens to the messages from loved ones to loved ones across the airways. He has learned a great deal by listening to these messages. "My God, the Palestinians seem to be everywhere except in Palestine," he thinks. Brothers in Kuwait, sisters in Saudi Arabia, aunts in America, uncles in a place called Australia, Libya, Britain, everywhere; the strange names of places he cannot even dream of or pronounce.

"My God, how did they scatter in this way? Who scattered them and how did they reach where they are now?"

He worries whether they are still Muslims or Christians or if all of them have turned Jewish. "Do they still speak Arabic? What of their children?" He thinks that regardless of what happens, he will never turn Jewish and hopes in his heart that no Palestinian has.

That is the only thing he ever liked to hear on the radio. His heart was too heavy for songs, and slowly but ever so surely, he began to mistrust almost everything else he heard on it. In any case, he does not understand most of it now, anyway. Not since that beating they gave him five years ago. He knows he lost something though he cannot tell what. He can tell by the way people look at him now, so strangely, as if they are afraid of him. At such times, he seems to be able to understand better than other times, as if acquiring an additional sense – the sense that animals in the wild have, someone told him. He laughs out loud and Amneh calls from inside: "Why are you laughing, Salem?" "Nothing, *ya marah*." He thinks he must control himself better in the future, for, he does not want to give Amneh additional worries. "Amneh my love, once my little kitten, what have I done to you?" Her hands are now like the bark of a tree from washing other people's clothes and their son Ahmad is now forever called *Ibn al-ghassaleh*, son of the washer-woman.

"And I, who wanted to do so much ended up with so little? What happened to my dreams, to my past, to my life, to my people?"

"Al-Bak'a, what a strange name." He wonders if it is a nice place with broad, beautiful streets, nice restaurants, like the ones he once saw in Jerusalem.

Why did the soldiers beat him? He cannot recall, but knows that he was passing by a crowd when he was dragged down and beaten. He thinks that he continued to scream for days, and that he felt his skull open and take in fresh air. It felt good at the time for he seemed not to worry any more, like now. Has he grown careless, like his wife says, lazy? No good? One thing he knows for sure and that is that he loves her, Ahmad and poor Handal, his daughter.

Why is it that whenever he thinks of Handal, he has to add "my daughter"? Is he reminding himself of something? That although she is grotesque she is still his flesh and blood? His eyes mist and he wonders at his constantly changing moods lately.

Another distraction. Handal coming back from wherever she had been. "Why can't I sleep so well lately? And these headaches!" It is not enough to tie a band of cloth around his head any more.

The blue sea, which is how he knows it, though some people have a name for it: *Al-Bahr Al-Abyad al-Mutawasit,* the Middle White Sea, the Mediterranean. It is so beautiful and he turns his radio on again.

A Kol Israel announcer is again quoting Yitzhak Shamir reiterating his often-repeated statement that Jerusalem is now the "eternal capital" of Israel. A capital "united" never to be divided again …

"What is eternal?" Salem wonders. And his eyes get misty while his smile broadens at the vain declaration.

"Harun Al-Rashid is now dust and so is Pharaoh. Even the holy men and prophets are dust. Nothing of them or their cities and places has remained. Am I crazy? Or is it that people never learn? Which is it? Or is it both? Likely both. The hell with Shamir."

The name always seems to stir up his emotions in a way he does not understand. "Amneh, bring me some tea."

"What? We have no sugar? Oh my God, what are we to drink tonight with our bread? And the neighbors surely cannot lend us any. Abu Mahmud is a good man, but he too has not found work for several days, and he has such a big family and his wife and mother are both ill. Maybe I should take them some bread this evening … or maybe they will be

91

insulted and I should not, or should I? Oh hell, never mind the tea. Eternal? Nothing is eternal."

"Shamir; the blue Mediterranean; the calm sea under the sun. Is the sun, our sun, mercy or curse?" he wonders.

As a young man he remembers stories told to him about the ancient *quinqueremes,* the Phoenician ships, the Roman galleons and the Arab boats from Sicily. He recalls the saying he once read on an old house in his village: 'Had it remained the property of those before, I would not have it now.' "Stupid bit of idle philosophizing, for, surely nothing but the face of God survives forever. Even imbeciles know that. Even I know that. Yet how can men, mere mortals, blaspheme about eternity? Everyone knows that four or five thousand years ago a Palestinian like myself sat on this very spot and was also, like me, worried about raising his family, his Amneh, Handal and Ahmad; a family like my family now. Surely they must have spoken a different language, looked or behaved differently, yet they were here and they are not here now – not even one trace of them is left.

"What does it matter what Shamir says? Mere words. For the substance underneath it all is the same and will remain the same till God changes things. God the changer that does not change."

He worries about that too, when he hears the staccato sound of a machine gun and much shooting. He does not pay any attention, though there is a lot of screaming. His mind wanders as he thinks, fifty or a hundred years from now none of this will remain. Fifty or a hundred years are eternal only for mortal human beings. A mortal's life is his eternity; nothing seems to stretch beyond that.

"What on earth is all that shooting?" And the noise is getting closer.

He thinks that Shamir too shall pass. "What is he? Yet another invader? Is this our winter?"

More shooting. It makes him sad, for he does not look forward to the impending struggle. That much his mind tells him and he knows it. More shooting as he hears Amneh scream and sees Handal fall and blood everywhere. He runs and then feels something warm, very warm enter his heart. He smiles as he falls over Handal and once more hears Amneh scream, and then peace. As his soul drifts away, I cannot but feel that life is truly *handal,* bitterness.

Somebody is doing his homework on the way home from school on
a wall that is made out of an oil barrel from the United Nation Relief
and works Agency for Palestine Refugees in the Near East (UNRWA)
in camp Baqa'a (pop. 55000), Jordan.

© 1980s UNRWA Photo By Munir Nasr

# Suleiman

Abu Hussein did not look exactly embarrassed, only a little troubled, as if reluctant to relate his story, perhaps especially in front of his wife. She, on the other hand, looked very interested, all ears, and kept smiling as if wishing to check what her husband would say.

"Suleiman, my husband," she said, "is very good at telling stories and he has some good ones to tell. Only make him, Doctor."

Suleiman, on the other hand, looked restless, a little uncomfortable and confused. Pushing his Arab head-dress to the back of his head with his left hand, he protested:

"I have no special story to tell. Like most Palestinians, that is my story: one day I had, and then another, I and my small family became itinerant wanderers on the streets. We stayed like that for a long time, I cannot, no; I do not want to remember how long. There is not much to tell: we walked, then we walked, and here we are, at last, I hope, settling down. That is all; we did what all other Palestinians did."

Um Hussein straightened her white headscarf and smiled. "No, that is not all," she said. "Tell him what you had to do along the way. Tell him the whole story from the beginning. You were young, Abu Hussein, and you did what you had to do. Do not be embarrassed, tell the Doctor."

Before settling down on the mattress on the floor, Suleiman pulled himself up to his full height of a little less than five feet and shook his head at his wife. "Woman, don't you know how to keep quiet? There are things that are best left untold." His small clear blue eyes looked troubled and his razor-thin white moustache appeared to be quivering. His upper lip looked broader than ever and his eyes again darted about.

"You don't have to tell your story," I said. "Oh no, but I do, I do otherwise you might think we have something to hide. We had to do what God, in His wisdom, wanted us to do." Suleiman then turned to his younger son Hassan and said" "Go make us some tea with mint and ask your sister, Fatimah, to come and listen." He added: "Maybe now that you have graduated from the university you will write this story down."

Under his bifocal glasses that made his eyes look larger, Hussein smiled. His paunch appeared to be shaking with the smile, and he said: "Father, your story is no different from others only my mother thinks it is and you should not believe her."

"Quiet," his father said. "You do not know anything, and now you sound like you know less since you graduated."

When Fatimah entered the room with Hassan, carrying a tray of glasses and the teapot, her father said: "Sit down, Fatimah, and listen as I tell our story to the Doctor." To me he turned and said: "She has a curious mind and never tires of hearing the story repeated. My boys do not care about it like her. She is clever."

Embarrassed and blushing at the words of praise, Fatimah shook my hand and sat down, quickly tucking her bare feet under her as she too settled on the mattress on the floor. She looked away as her father began.

"We, the Shawahis, are not only a very large family, but also an old and a good one. My grandfather used to say that one of our ancestors was a companion of the Prophet. Now that we only barely manage, of course you cannot tell and, in fact, now even my children snicker when I say that, but I am telling you. In our village, only 14 kilometers from Gaza City, which was also called Gazit Hashim, since Hashim, the grandfather of the Prophet was buried in it, we used to be a respected and well-to-do family. My father owned his own house and over four hundred *dunams* of land. And in the enclosure around it, we had a vegetable garden and a small stable that housed his horse, a few milking sheep and goats, the ploughing mules, chickens. On the roof we kept the pigeons.

"We never bought bread like I do today. In those days it was a shame for people to buy their bread like beggars from the market. People used to bake their own bread every day and so did my mother in the hearth oven in the corner of the yard. That was bread, real wheat bread, and not like we buy now, made from American flour. This does not even taste like bread, but what can we do?"

Here, his wife interjected: "Thank God, Suleiman, that we have it; it is a blessing that we have it, and you should not talk like that in front of the children."

"Quiet," he said. "You know I always thank God for His gifts." And then he resumed.

"I said we were a very large family; my father was one of the 14 sons of his father. I do not know how many daughters he had, but I was my father's only son and I had eight sisters from the three wives he married. Only five of my sisters are now alive. They are, like the rest of the Shawahis, scattered around the world. One lives in Shneller refugee camp with her children, her husband died two years ago. She is doing well, one of her children is a taxi-driver and another is a high school teacher in the UNRWA school. We visit her and her family often and yes, we are good friends. My second sister and her husband went to America some years ago, to a country called Brazil and we never hear from her. Two of my sisters are married and with their families in Kuwait, and the eldest sister lives near us with her husband and family in al-Nasr refugee camp in Amman. Of course we are scattered, but thank God we are all alive and doing well.

"How did I get here? When did we leave? I cannot tell for sure. It is a long story that is maybe not interesting. Are you sure you want to hear it?"

Here he got some coins out of his pocket and asked his son Hassan to go and buy some cookies to go with the tea. Hassan protested vigorously, he wanted to hear the story, but his mother sternly admonished him: "Boy, listen to your father. Shame on you, go and get the cookies now."

His father shook his head vigorously. "New generation, they do not listen to anyone anymore. Spoiled, I suppose. It is a shame, but I have too much heart, I think, at least that is what Um Hussein says. Well, anyway, since I was my father's only son, he had me get married very young. I was only 15 at the time. Um Hussein was only 13 and she was my cousin, daughter of my uncle on my mother's side. We got married in 1947, in the autumn of 1947. It was a beautiful wedding. My father slaughtered many sheep and for seven nights the festivities went on: that was the way it was in those days. My father wanted to see my fruit, my progeny. Poor man, he died only a few weeks later of a heart attack. I think … I think sometimes he was lucky; he never lived to see what happened. My mother died in the war, the war of 1948 of course. A stray bullet, who knows? It could have been a Zionist, an Egyptian or a Palestinian commando bullet. She, too, I think was lucky to die so … so quickly, and at that time before all the humiliation and the exodus. And now here we are. For God's sake, see if you can find me a job, any job, Doctor.

"We did not know when the war started – in our village we had no radios in those days – but all of a sudden there was the Egyptian army and very soon we learned that it was surrounded by the Zionist army. I do not know how that happened and I do not know of anyone that knows either. The Egyptian army was commanded by a brave man whom we used to call the black hyena. I also saw Jamal – *Bikbasha* Jamal, Captain Jamal – you know, Jamal Abdel Nasser who later became the president of Egypt. Of course, we liked the Egyptians and helped them and the people liked Jamal. I was told later by those who knew him then that he was always angry. It was because the corrupt King Farouk gave them bad weapons.

"I remember, of course I remember, for six months we were besieged along with the Egyptian army and then, one day, United Nations observers appeared and we, and the Egyptian army, were allowed to withdraw. My wife, she is clever, she hid her gold bracelets on her and we marched with all our fellow villagers towards Gaza. Some of the old or sick were able to ride on the United Nations trucks, but I and Um

Hussein and all others walked. It was a dusty, dirty walk, and a very long one, too. I was still a groom, and she was only a young bride, a baby, and I felt like crying, many times, but would not, not in front of her.

"We reached Gaza. I have no idea why the Gazans like it; from the moment I laid eyes on it, I took a dislike to it. To this day I still dislike it. It does not look like the rest of Palestine and it reminds me of the Jews that took our land. Well, the UNRWA people gave us a small tent and some blankets, but I hated to see my young wife in one. Many of us were like that and a group of us decided we should leave, and soon. A few weeks later, a group of us simply left our tents and walked out, heading for the city of Abraham the friend, friend of God, Hebron. It is called thus because our father, Ibrahim, [Abraham] was the friend of God [*khalil allah*]. God used to speak with him all the time, and now he sits near the throne of God, on his right side. We thought, if anywhere, God would not abandon us there. You see, we Muslims, we bless our Father Ibrahim and his progeny – we are his progeny – at least five times a day, at every one of our daily prayers.

"Though we had little food, we took only the blankets. Soon we ran out of food. Although 15 and married, I looked very young and some of the men and women in our group persuaded me, along with some other boys, to go and beg for some bread from al-Dahriyyah village near al-Khalil [Hebron]. I did, and was never so ashamed in my whole life, never. That is the shameful thing my wife is referring to. But she had to eat, I and the others had to eat and there was no work; what was I to do? One man from the village recognized us: 'You are Shawahis, aren't you. My God, and you turned beggars. What has happened to these times? But don't worry, it is only a cloud that will soon pass, soon you will go back.'

"My God, 42 years have passed, and now we are further away from going back than ever. Damn the Arab governments – all of them – and damn Shamir too. He is so short and ugly, but he can win against all of them, all of our leaders, including Abu Ammar. Yes, I am ashamed to say it, but I begged; but what else could I have done?

"We could not stay in al-Khalil; the town was crowded and there was no work, and soon we were on the road again. We stayed one day in Jerusalem and then headed for a refugee camp near Jericho. My God, it was hot even in winter. It was there that we found some of our relatives, who made room for us in their tent. God, I hate tents. On one side they made room for me and my wife. She was still a bride and used to cry a lot.

"Life has not been easy, but then, perhaps I am luckier than many other Palestinians. You see, now I own my own home, which I built from my own sweat, not anybody else's, and not inherited. I have come to love Amman: it is where my children, all my children, Hussein, Hassan and Fatimah were born. King Hussein is nice. What is he to do alone if all the other Arabs cannot fight? Sometimes I think Abu Ammar is too harsh on Hussein."

Looking at his son, Hussein, he said: "Pour some more tea for the Doctor. Drink, it is nice. Maybe you need some more sugar. My children sometimes forget their manners; I have to remind them how they should treat their guests."

His narrow blue eyes seemed to come closer together as he continued: "I am very old, about as old as you, Doctor, but I forgot to tell you that while in al-Khalil I took my wife and visited the Mosque of Abraham. We prayed over the soul of al-Khalil [friend of God, Abraham] and his wife Sarah, and the other members of the Ibrahimi [Abrahamic] family. I would like to go back and visit it one day.

"Well, soon I found a day job with a construction company building roads for the government, expanding the road between Jericho and Amman. And soon, along with my job, my family and I drifted to Amman.

"For nearly 40 years I lived in al-Nasr refugee camp. That is how I survived. It was hard in the beginning, cold, sometimes with little to eat, sometimes with nothing but the clothes that others threw away or those I bought cheap at the second-hand clothes stores around the camp. Until this day, I was never able once, not once, to buy a new jacket. Maybe when Hussein gets a job, he will buy me one. Can you help him, Doctor, to get a job in the Gulf; they give better pay there, can you? It is your brother, Doctor, who gave me this jacket. I like it though it is several sizes too large. Your brother also sold me this piece of land and, God bless him, he sold it to me cheap. He gave me a deal and I, in turn, help him to sell some of the other pieces he still has nearby at regular prices. I have already helped sell three pieces. God always gives and he never forgets his slaves. Like all humans, I, too, am his slave.

"I still owe some money from building the house and it eats most of the retirement pension I get from my former job. I worked as an office boy, you know, carrying papers around from office to office in the department, delivering coffee or tea to the office clerks, sometimes doing some of them favors. I lived, I saved, and I educated Hussein. He graduated from the University of Jordan, he studied business administration and graduated two months ago. Help us find him a job, please.

"Fatimah, she is clever, God bless her. She has graduated from high school and is now studying to be a seamstress. She liked and wanted that, and I hope that her fortune in marriage will be good. Two of her cousins wanted her, but I refused: they were not educated like her, not good enough.

"Hassan, too, finished government high school and is now waiting to be called for national service, which is good. You see, he does not want to go to the university like his elder brother and he hopes that in the army he will be able to learn a trade: car mechanic, cook, well, something. What can I do?

"You see, Doctor, there is nothing shameful in my life. My children have never lived like I lived in Palestine, but they too love their country. Hussein is sure that one of these days we will all go back. Me, I will never go back if and when they can go back. Me? I have done enough travelling for one man in one lifetime. I love my house, and Palestine or no Palestine, I will not walk again. Hussein, Hassan and Fatimah, God bless the original children of the Prophet, and mine named after them, they can go. They can walk; they can do anything they want. I have educated them. But me and Um Hussein, we will stay put here. Nothing will ever move us again, not even if Shamir and his army, God forbid, march on us again."

UNRWA suspended general ration distribution to Palestine refugees in 1982 except to families living in hardship conditions. This eligible family in Jalazone camp receives welfare assistance from UNRWA to aid with food and shelter repairs.

© 1982 UNRWA Archive Photo by Munir Nasir

# Ali

It was in Australia that I met Ali. I had been there for about a week, attending the twenty-fifth anniversary celebrations of the Australian Institute of International Affairs, when someone told me that I must see Ali. A week later, at a dinner hosted by the Jordanian ambassador to Australia, I was told by someone else that I should meet Ali. On this occasion, the ambassador enthusiastically endorsed the idea and offered to arrange the meeting, over a cup of coffee, next day in his office. "His is the story of Palestinian success in the diaspora," the ambassador asserted, "and now that he is so involved in the affairs of the Arab community of Australia, you will surely wish to know this man."

He added: "Ali is not only a prominent businessman and philanthropist, but has some very good contacts with Australian officials at the highest level as well."

My colleague and I met Ali the following day in the ambassador's office, where we had a good chat and exchanged views regarding Arab and Palestinian affairs, not only in the "old country" [the Middle East] but also in the *mahjar*, the new home of the émigrés.

"The Arab, including the Palestinian community, is prosperous in Australia," Ali said, then added: "But as usual, they are just as divided and disorganized as ever, with mini-communities for the Lebanese, the Egyptians, the Palestinians and even the Jordanians. When they meet, more often than not, they end up arguing. Always on the verge of a fight, what is wrong with us, Professor? Why cannot we get together like the Jews do? There are more Arabs in Australia than Jews, but the Jews are infinitely more effective. Here, it is like in America, they control public opinion and are very influential in government."

It was on our way to his farm, about 100 kilometers to the north of Canberra, that I finally induced him to tell his story. Where did he come from? How did he end up living in Canberra? What did he do here? How did he feel about his life in the new world? Did he have a family?

Driving his sleek Mercedes-Benz 280 along the Australian highway, he resembled anything but a Palestinian refugee. Prosperity suited his gentle looks, dark wavy hair and piercing black eyes. Sporting a thin moustache, already streaked with white, he appeared as if born into his rich surroundings. Neither flashy in dress nor in speech, he kept repeating that it was God's bounty and his parents' blessings. "The blessings of my parents, Doctor, that is why I never felt lonely either here or in Germany. That is why I have no anger and hatred in me. Even the Jews, and after all they did to us, to me, I do not hate, and I am proud to say that I have very good relations with some of them here. They too, like us, are victims of circumstance. Anyway I am too busy to hate, and I hope that one day we will achieve peace.

"I was born in a small village near Yafa, Palestine. I do not remember anything about it except I keep thinking it was beautiful and that it was once my land. My father and mother, sisters and brothers became refugees overnight. To this day I do not know how. One day we were in our house and the next we found ourselves on the road. It is a road that seems to have no end. Do you remember, Doctor, when we were little, the old ones would tell us a story that almost always included ghosts, sorcerers and a road 'that takes but never brings back'? This is how I always feel, a wanderer on the road that goes away and never returns. And this is spite of my blessings, thank God.

"I remember we moved from camp to camp. Each time my father died a little more, and one day we found ourselves in al-Hussein camp in Amman. My father and older brother did the odd jobs they could find and skin and bone were kept together. People now find it fashionable to curse the UNRWA, but without it we could have never survived. One thing my mother insisted on was that I, of all my brothers and sisters, go to school, and I did … I graduated from high school and started looking for a job. There were no jobs in Amman in those days, in the late fifties, but with the help of a friend I finally got one. The pay was very low, but it helped the family and gave me dignity and hope.

"Hope. It was hope that kept me and my friend alive. We used to sit and discuss our future plans by the hour, for ourselves, our families, and our Palestine. And one day we decided to save money so that one of us could emigrate to Germany. We heard there were lots of work opportunities, and the visa restrictions were not so harsh and time-consuming as the American. I never thought of Australia then. Who would? So far away. It took a long time, a little over two years of scrimping and saving, to get enough money for my friend to go to Germany. All our friends, unaware of what we were doing, thought we were cheap misers for we would not go to a café, cinema or anywhere with them.

"As planned, my friend, Adnan, went to Germany and within a few months he sent me the price of the airline ticket and some money to come and join him. In the meanwhile, my father died. My mother's heart died with him. She began to dry up like an uprooted flower right before our eyes. Only her eyes kept their luster, the rest of her lost its color like an old cloth left out in the sun. She never sang again after he died. It was not a long time after I left for Germany that she, too, died. My brother wrote to me that she was happy to die, hopelessness having settled on her heart like a weight.

"I could never do anything right in Germany and I drifted from job to job, each time swearing that the next one would be better and more permanent. Each time I found myself on the street seeking another job and I began, again with my friend, Adnan, to think of emigrating, to Australia. Everything I heard about Australia then turned out to be true. A fresh, clean, virgin country, unspoiled by the ancient hatreds and animosities that are the hallmarks of the old world. Adnan and I would sit hour after hour dreaming of Australia, scheming how to get there. And again we saved, and now that I had purpose, I found I could keep a job better. One day we saved enough so that I could go. This time I went first.

"The trip on the ship was delightful. Looking back on it today, and though I love my wife and children, those days on the ship were the happiest days of my life. But they were so short. One of these days, when I have time, I will travel on a ship again. And then the trip ended and another reality began. I knew no English. I had picked up a few phrases and words in German, but they were of no use in Australia. But, Doctor, from the moment I laid eyes on Australia I fell in love. I fell in love with the city of Sydney, with the land and with the people. Somehow, Doctor, not only my eyes but my heart also opened up. God bless, I said. And God blessed indeed.

"Walking down the gangplank with my small cloth suit-case in my hand, I remembered I had in my pocket only a few German pfennigs, coins of small value, and I stopped, took them out of my pocket and dumped them into the sea. In my heart I prayed. God is great; these coins can do me no good here. I also wanted to enter Australia completely clean so that one day when I related the story to my children, I would be telling the truth, that I entered Australia clean broke, not a coin of any denomination from any country in my pockets.

"And that is how I stepped onto Australian soil. I only knew a few words of English, what remained of my studies in school. There was no one to meet me and all of a sudden I felt a terrible loneliness for home, for Palestine. What am I doing here, I thought. But the mood quickly passed as I carried my bag and wondered which way to turn, left or right, and in my disorientation I started walking back and forth on one of the back streets parallel to the pier. No language, no money, no friends and nowhere to go. I must have walked back and forth on the same street several times when I heard someone calling me, not by name, only 'Hey, hey. You there.'

"An old Australian with a very pink face was sitting on his porch on a rocking chair, and apparently he had been watching me for some time. No, I do not remember how long, but I noticed then that the sun was well into the late afternoon. It was over tea that he made clear to me, with the few phrases of English I knew and much gesturing, that he understood my predicament. The man was kind, a true human being he was. I do not know if he is still alive. 'Don't worry,' the Australian said and he took me in his car to a place that turned out to be a philanthropic society to aid newly arrived immigrants into the country. He left me there and I have never looked him up again. I am ashamed of myself for that.

"Oh yes, the society is still there and now I am one of its major sponsors. I also sponsor several other such societies in Australia. No, I do not care who they help, whether it is an Arab or not. You see, they did not know me, but they gave me a clean, small room, food and even a little pocket money and they told me I could stay with them till I found a job. And then if and when I wanted to or could, it was up to me to pay them back. They did not ask me to pay them back, only if and when I wanted to.

"What has happened to me since? Well, it was a climb, and God in his mercy took my hand. I had many jobs: taxi-driver, porter, waiter, and janitor working in a supermarket. One day, God looked upon me, and I decided to sell vegetables on the side of a highway, just a few boxes of lettuce, tomatoes and squash. God blessed the venture and everything I touched turned into gold. It must be the blessings and the contentment of my parents. I kept in touch with my family, though soon after I left my mother followed the old man. They are now both in the house of God.

"The vegetable stand eventually turned into a shop, then a supermarket, and then several supermarkets. And then I sold them and moved into farming and the import-export business, as well as investing in a variety of economic enterprises in Australia and Singapore. Now I am one of the major suppliers of fresh and frozen red meat to the Gulf states and Saudi Arabia. Mostly sheep. I have two farms now, the one I am taking you to, which is the smaller of the two and about 6,000 hectares with about six or seven thousand sheep, and a larger one much further away. In this small farm, I have only my brother and an Australian, both work only part time. You do not need to worry about the sheep in Australia, they need no shepherd. You see, Doctor, this is a blessed land that does not have any natural predators in it, so everybody lets their sheep roam in the wild and they are wild." Here he laughed and I asked why.

"Well, it is a funny story in a way. The first shipment of my sheep reached one of the Gulf countries and the importer there was waiting at the port with some shepherds. When I told him these were wild sheep, that they would not follow shepherds and that they needed to be driven directly into pens or transported in trucks, he did not believe me. 'Sheep are sheep everywhere and I have some very good shepherds with me. Just release the sheep and we will take care of the rest,' he said. Nothing would convince him, and when the sheep hit the ground, they scattered like wild deer all over the place. I have no idea how many of them he retrieved.

"That is my life. God gave to me and now I am married to my cousin, and we have several children. We go to the old country [the Middle East] together every two or three years. My children, like me, are Palestinians at heart. That is something I want them to be. They speak some Arabic and they are active in the Palestinian community here, and I do what I can. Of course, I contribute to the PLO and I contribute to every Arab activity that touches on Palestine. Sometimes even my wife, who is also Palestinian, thinks I am too sentimental, that I have romanticized it all but I cannot help myself. No, I am not atoning for not going back by paying and contributing, I would like to die here in Australia where I have put down roots, and I tell my children that now this is their home and future. But I would like to die with the thought that though I could not do what I should have, at least I may be of help to someone who can.

"I know that Palestine is not only for the Palestinians alone, but for all the Arabs and the world of Islam. I never told you, Doctor, did I, that I am a Palestinian Turkoman. My father was one of the remnants of the Ottoman army that withdrew from Palestine at the end of World War I. He did that out of choice. My father loved Palestine, and he settled along the shores of the Mediterranean, at a now forgotten village that the Zionists blew up to establish one of their own colonies. He wanted to be a neighbor of Jerusalem and its environs. And though now I live in Australia and will never go back except for visits, I too think of myself as a neighbor of Jerusalem, and my mind's eye sees it once in a while."

After more than 20 years of military occupation, a spontaneous popular uprising in the West Bank and the Gaza Strip begins. Israel enacts house demolition policies upon individual accused of taking part in the first intifada. Ahmed Mas'our Safi, an UNRWA camp serves officer, lives in Jalazone camp in the West Bank. Here, he shows what remains of his home, demolished two days after being released from serving nine months of detention without charge.

House demolitions are one way Israeli authorities punish and deter those convicted or suspected of security offences in Gaza Strip and West Bank. Other methods of deterrence include detention, fine, imprisonment and the sealing of rooms. Here children play atop the ruins of a demolished house in Jalazone cam, West Bank.

© UNRWA photo G.Nehmeh

# Jamal

Um Jamal had a hearty laugh. "Why, of course," she said, "I love to tell my story. No, Jamal cannot remember. He was only four years old at the time. A beautiful baby with a big smile."

I was talking to her on the telephone, while Jamal was listening and looking uncomfortable as I was talking to his mother, checking on some small details of his life story. "Abu Jamal, Jamal's father, was a nice man who liked everything in order. He was the warden of a young boys' reformatory he had established, and headed many in Palestine and, after the 1948 disaster, in Jordan too. He was a very kind and nice man. He even spoke English," she said with much pride in her voice. I wondered how she looked now, in her late sixties.

Jamal was definitely looking very uncomfortable now. The conversation with his mother was taking much longer than he had anticipated and he was probably wondering what his mother was telling me. Maybe, in her innocence, she was telling me something that he did not want revealed.

It was early on a cool July morning in my garden in Amman, a cool breeze blowing from the west gently stirring the trees and flowers around us. Sitting under our grape-vine, the atmosphere and the early morning hour had little to do with the tragedy of Palestine and the Palestinians. At that moment, Jerusalem seemed as far away as the other side of the moon.

Jamal began fidgeting, then got up and started walking about in the garden – a sure signal that he was not only bored but annoyed as well. He had given me his mother's telephone number to check on a minor detail in his story, but the conversation was taking too much time. I decided to hastily thank her after asking her permission to phone again or, better yet, pay her a visit. "Why, of course, any time," she said and hung up.

As Jamal returned to his chair he looked relieved, perhaps even pleased that the conversation with his mother had finally ended. His youthful face revealed nothing of his age, nor the turbulence of his early years.

"It was an uphill struggle all the way," he said. "And now, sitting with you under this grape-vine, in this garden and trying to remember, it seems many of the things that happened in my life happened to someone else. I cannot believe that I was ever insecure, struggling and in need. Thank God, now I am affluent, definitely rich by comparison with the memories of my youth ... my youth during which my family and I spent moving from place to place. First in Lebanon, and then when we moved to Jordan, in Jordan itself. It is Nablus that I remember most. We lived a comparatively long time there and in a way it has become my town too.

"No, I come from Tirat Haifa, only 12 kilometers from Haifa. I do not remember anything about it. I never visited it, and the Israelis have since razed the village to the ground; completely erased it from the face of the earth. In its place now, I am told, are high-rise buildings and suburbs of Haifa."

A cloud passed over his face when he added: "You see, the Israelis raze Palestinian villages and replace them with settlements, so when a Palestinian returns even on a short visit, he can never find what was once his village nor can he relate in any way to the new modern colony.

"I also consider myself a Jerusalemite, having been born in the Muscovite Hospital there. It is ironic that when the Israelis first arrested me I was incarcerated in the Muscovite prison in Jerusalem. My father was a nice man who wanted very much to go to college but could not, because of circumstances. His father, my grandfather, was a comparatively well-to-do man with a grocery shop in Haifa and land that he farmed in al-Tirah. He sent my father to finish the English High School in Brumanah, Lebanon. When my grandfather was arrested by the British in the 1936-39 Palestine revolt, my father had to terminate his studies and return home to take care of the family while my grandfather was in jail.

"My father got himself a clerical job in the Mandatory Government of Palestine. It was easy for him to get the job since he spoke good English. He was eventually promoted to the post of warden of the boy's reformatory in Acca. He kept the job till we were forced to migrate in 1948. I cannot remember these events, though I can, in my mind's eye, visualize them. We moved to Lebanon because my father knew Lebanon, he had studied there.

"Later my mother told me she had brought with her only a large can of white cheese and about 2,000 Palestinian pounds – my father's life savings. The mother of Rajih, now a prominent Jordanian public figure, tagged along with my family I have no idea how she came along with us, but she and my mother were good friends. She was very confused at the time, you know, our people were afraid for their women's honor. We heard so many ugly stories of how the Zionists abused Palestinian women.

"Of course, I do not remember, I told you that, and you checked it out with my mother, didn't you." He was almost annoyed as he said that and I was afraid he would stop. But he did not. Continuing his tale, he said: "The people of al-Tirah are not reputed to be very smart. It is said that when the sea becomes rough, they shoot at it to keep it calm. Anyway, many of the inhabitants of our village started moving to our house in Acca, especially following the fall of Yafa, and then Haifa, to the Jews. I remember now, they did not completely change the name of our village, the place is now called Tirat Ha Carmel, as it lies at the foot of Haifa's Mount Carmel." He stopped and I recalled his mother's story, earlier on the telephone:

"We left very early in the morning with my husband's folks who had come the night before, running away from the bombardment of the village. On my arm I carried my baby daughter, born only ten days earlier. *Silfi* [my brother-in-law], who used to work in the British camp near Haifa, persuaded a British truck driver to transport us to Ras al-Naqurah, on the border with Lebanon. Abu Jamal refused to accompany us, he insisted on staying to hand over the material and household furniture and effects of the *islahiyyeh* [reformatory] to the government. You see, he was a very legal man and he could not just leave without everything being legal. When a month passed and no British official appeared to receive the material entrusted to him, he finally left Acca and followed us to Lebanon.

"We lived a few terrible nights on the border. The Lebanese would not let us into Lebanon with the river of refugees pouring in, as we had come to the border in a British truck. When we, I, finally convinced them we did not work with the British, they offered to let us in, but we could not find any means of transportation so I had to ride alone with a friend from the Mahdi family of Haifa all the way to Sur, Tyre, and there hire two taxis at exorbitant prices to bring them back to the border checkpoint. When we finally reached Tyre, we could not find a place to rent: no rooms, no hotels, nothing. Then someone advised us to move to a small village, Juwayyeh, nearby where we found a small house – really a shelter, with no electricity, no running water, nothing. It was terrible.

"It was from this house that I sent a message to my husband, who joined us later. In addition to the can of cheese and the money, I took with me only the baby's clothes. To this day I feel sad that we had to leave some personal effects left with us in Acca by a friend when he fled from Haifa earlier. It is bad enough to lose your own possessions, but worse still to lose a trust left by a friend.

"Abu Jamal was adamant about going back to Acca to hand over the reformatory effects. One day he went to the garage in Tyre to take a taxi back to Acca and learned that Acca too had fallen to the Jews. He refused to remain in Juwayyeh, and though heartbroken, he decided we should move to the village of Seer al-Dhniyyah, near Tarablus [Tripoli], in north Lebanon. He knew the village and there we spent the remainder of the summer in the hope that the Arab armies would recapture Acca and we would return. You see, we are still waiting, after 45 years." It was Jamal who filled in the next stage of the story.

"In Tarablus, my father soon found a job with UNRWA. It was easy for him since he was educated. He was made responsible for the social conditions in the Palestinian refugee camps. From this experience, my father, to the last day of his life, often repeated to us: 'You see, education is more valuable than anything else in life. You can carry it with you wherever you go. What good now is the shop, the land, even the olive trees we used to have?' It is a lesson that I shall never forget and one that I shall pass on to my children and their children's children too, if I can.

"It was in 1952 that the Jordanian government asked my father to come to Jordan and take charge of the *islahyyeh* of Bethlehem, and that is how we moved to the West Bank, then part of the Kingdom of Jordan. Later, the government transferred my father to al-Khalil, Hebron, then to Ramallah, then to Irbid, then to Amman and then to Nablus, all in a matter of two years; and each time to set up a centre for social affairs or an *islahyyeh*.

"When, in 1956, the government once again transferred my father to Irbid, he went for two months and then threatened to resign if not returned to Nablus, a request which was finally granted. You see, my father was worried about my education. In Nablus I became a very good student, always the first in my class. We remained in Nablus till I graduated from high school and won an UNRWA scholarship to study at the American University of Beirut, in Lebanon. It was in Lebanon that I became involved in the Arab National Movement. Gamal

Abdel Nasser's influence on me was immense; the man offered a ray of hope.

"I graduated in 1965 and continued my studies for my master's degree, which I received in 1967. I had to get a job and I worked with Dr. Fayes Sayegh in the Palestine Research Centre. Dr. Sayegh, too, had a great influence on me. I became highly politicized, what with the establishment of the Palestine Liberation Organization in 1964 and the glimmer of hope it offered. I became president of the Palestinian Students Union in Lebanon and chairman of the Arab Student Federation, too. We talked a lot, we made speeches, we marched; that was part of my upbringing, too. My hand was always on my heart for Palestine, and when the 1967 war broke out, we cheered. We believed in our cause, in Abdel Nasser, in the Arab armies.

"Five hundred Arab students and I went to Syria to volunteer for the war effort. The Syrians lodged us at the foot of Mount Qasiyun. A couple of days later, myself and only about 80 other students, mostly Palestinians and Jordanians, moved to Jordan to help with the war effort. We camped in the village of Sweileh, to the west of Amman. It was only here that we learned of the Arab defeat from the returning Jordanian soldiers, some of whom were still crying. We too were crushed.

"I was facing another difficulty. You see, I was being sought out by the intelligence service in Jordan. I could not remain there, so I managed to run away to Syria and from there to Lebanon, where I joined forces once again with Dr. George Habash. With Habash we established the resistance group later called the Popular Front for the Liberation of Palestine [PFLP], and I recently moved back to Jordan to recruit for the organization.

"It was on a cold night in December 1967 that I and another four commandos crossed the Jordan River into occupied Palestine. At that time the water reached my neck; what has happened to the water of the river?"

To his question I could have answered that the Israelis have diverted most of it to irrigate their vegetable farms in the Negev desert, but instead I let him continue his story. He went on:

"After we crossed the river, we joined forces with a band of sugar and rice smugglers stealing into the West Bank. Eventually we were engaged by an Israeli border patrol and three of us were killed, while a couple of my comrades and I succeeded in reaching Ramallah where we got in touch with our contact.

"Later I moved to Jerusalem and I took *ismi al-haraki* [*nom de guerre*]. I was in an unfurnished room in old Jerusalem when I was arrested and taken to the Muscovite prison. Felicia Langer, you have heard of her, the famous Jewish lawyer, defended. She wrote about me in her book *With My Own Eyes,* cataloguing Israeli atrocities and human rights violations against the Palestinians. She gave her book this title as she witnessed, with her own eyes, the abuses committed by the Israelis against us.

"Later I was sentenced to a prison term of a year and a half on the charge of stealing back into Palestine. Because I was the president of the Palestinian Students Union my case received worldwide publicity; also because I was the first graduate of the American University of Beirut to be arrested and tried.

"In October of 1968 the Israeli authorities decided to deport me to Jordan. Before going, I asked them to permit me to visit my grandparents, then still alive in Jerusalem, a request that they surprisingly granted. I never saw them again, a couple of years later both died, alone and heart-broken, without any family around them. The Israelis took me to the bridge, the King Hussein Bridge that they still insist on calling the Allenby Bridge, with my eyes blindfolded. After a bumpy ride in the back of a truck, I was suddenly in the middle of the bridge, faced by a moustachioed Jordanian soldier asking my name.

"Of course the conditions in the Israeli jails were terrible. They moved me from al-Moscobiyyeh to the old Ramleh prison, then to the terrible Sarafand prison camp, back to Ramleh prison and again back to Sarafand prison for torture, and then to Ramallah prison. The food was terrible, I lost 16 kilos in jail and I was afraid I had contracted tuberculosis, but thank God, that did not happen. As you see, I have regained it; in fact, I am now watching my weight.

"The Jordanian police took me from the bridge and I was transported to Amman for interrogation. They did not abuse me, they wanted to know. I told them my story, and at the end of the day they released me. I was contacted to re-enlist in the PFLP, but I was tired and disillusioned because of the split in the front. In January 1970 I abandoned the Palestinian armed struggle.

"What to do next? Where to go? I needed badly to continue my studies, but where? A friend, long since killed by the Israelis for working with Dr. Wadi Haddad's group, helped me. An Arab professor at a Canadian university helped secure a place, while another friend paid for my travel to Canada. Of course I offered to pay him after I graduated and got my first job, but he refused. He told me: 'Help someone else.' Sometimes I do, when I can.

"In Canada I worked my way to my Ph.D., working mostly at the university, and these were some of the happiest days of my life. In 1973, I returned to Lebanon, where in the meantime my mother had started working as a seamstress in a small firm. Then she established her own shop, which she still operates. She was paying for my younger brother's education in the Soviet Union and my sister's at the Beirut Women's College near the AUB. I helped when I could.

"When a general amnesty was declared by King Hussein, following the 1973 Arab summit meeting in Alexandria, I returned to Jordan, but because of lack of work I returned to Beirut to work again in the Palestine Research Centre for the same salary I had received before I got my Ph.D. I had to do it, I had to live. Then I got a job teaching in Kuwait, where I remained for some time, after which I returned to Jordan and assumed my present position."

It was at this juncture that he scratched his head and smiled. "My God," he said, "I did not know that so many things happened in my life, one tends to forget, especially the difficult times. Only now, after talking to you, do I realize how turbulent and difficult my life was. People look at me now, even I look at myself that way every now and then, and think that I have lived all my life in luxury." That is how he ended his story, luxury for him being the modest rented flat he lives in and the not-too-new Japanese car he drives. Luxury, though, indeed it is, what with his lovely smiling wife and his beautiful children, two of them, twins just learning how to walk.

Jamal did not dwell on the torture he received in Israeli jails, nor on his longing for Palestine. He did not swear anything, neither return, nor revenge, though his highly polished will shone through when he added: "My children will carry my memories of the Palestine I hardly saw or knew, but it is alive for me and so it shall be for them."

As he said this, there was no bitterness in his voice, only quiet dignity and resolve. He did not dwell on the terrible conditions of Israeli jails, on how he had to stay in solitary confinement in his cell of less than one meter in width, length and height, where he had to crouch most of the time with his knees under his chin listening to the screams of the other Palestinians being tortured night and day. He did not tell of the tens of thousands of Palestinian youths in the horrible Israeli detainee camps of al-Ansar, many of whom never see the light of day for weeks on end, nor did he tell of the physical and mental scars that the Israeli atrocities left on his nation, or of the thousands of Palestinians who have already perished, or the children now perishing at the hands of the Israelis since the Intifada.

Jamal's smile was sad as he rushed away saying: "Please excuse me, peace be with you. See you later." He did not tell of his other accomplishments, the books and articles he has written for Arab and international journals, nor did he tell what was in his heart for the future. There were many questions left and issues to be discussed, but Jamal declared that he had remembered more than he cared to remember for one day.

Maybe one day, when the olive trees of Palestine are not being uprooted by Israeli bulldozers and can grow healthily again.

It was also then that I recalled the terrible impact left on me by the story related by a Palestinian professor in an interview on Jordan Television, in which he said how, in the many years he had spent in jail, the Israelis never once allowed him to use a mirror. "I forgot how I looked and when I saw myself after being released I was shocked. I had almost lost my identity. I was shocked to see the man facing me in the mirror and I had to remind myself that it was myself and no one else."

Ghor Nimreen was the biggest of six emergency tented camps
established for new refugees in the Jordan Valley in the autumn of 1967.
Following military action along the Jordan River in February 1968, the
inhabitants moved to new camps in the hills north of Amman, Jordan.

UNRWA Photo No. RW-Shufat-8, Winter snow cover Shufat
refugees camp, near Jerusalem in the West Bank Shufat camp in
which 4,000 Palestine refugees are registered with UNRWA, lies just
north of Jerusalem in the Israeli occupied West Bank .The camps was
build in 1966 to re-house inhabitants of Mu'ascar camp which was
located in the old dirt of Jerusalem.

© UNRWA photo by Myrle Winter Chaumeny, 77577

# Ra'd

Ra'd's father looked relaxed, almost pleased with himself, as he greeted me in his traditional living room: deep green velour overstuffed seats, an imitation Persian rug on the floor, a large dining table in one corner, and the traditional mattress on the other side of the room.

For the occasion of meeting me in his home, Abu Ra'd had dressed in a honey-colored *aba* over a similarly colored *dishdash* [Arab man's robe], and the Arab head-dress as well. He looked handsome and dignified in spite of at least two days' unshaved stubble.

He greeted me with a formal but warm welcome, and soon afterwards his grandson, Ahab entered the room and sat opposite his grandfather. Ahab was obviously interested in my visit, of which he had learned not only from his grandfather but also from the owner of the laundry next to their house. After all, I had come to inquire about the circumstances of the death – no, the martyrdom – of his uncle Ra'd two years ago. Though only 11, Ahab was not only knowledge-able about his uncle's *shahadeh* [martyrdom] but very proud of it as well. During my conversation with his grandfather, he frequently interjected a comment, a correction, prompting his grandfather to say, "*uskut ya walad*", [Quiet, boy] or "What do you know?" and finally, "Go and tell your grandmother to make us some tea."

Ra'd's story is a simple one: there is really not much to tell … how complicated can a life that ended at 19 be? "For him it should have been only spring," said Abdul Karim, Ra'd's father.

Coffee arrived, instead of tea, and my host wanted to know why. Ahab flippantly answered: "How should I know? Ask my grandmother why she made coffee instead of tea."

Abdul Karim looked as if he was going to say that ordinarily coffee comes at the end, not the beginning of a visit, then thought better of it and turned to me to ask: "And what can I tell you about my Ra'd?"

"On Wednesday night, two nights before the operation, he came home early from the mosque, bathed and shaved. You see, although he was very religious, very devout, he did not have a beard. He was a private person, almost a recluse, and always kept to himself. That evening after his bath, he looked beautiful in my eyes. I never saw anything more beautiful in my life … I can still see him now, so clean, so young, so innocent, and I tell you, Doctor, something I have never told anyone before … I said to myself that evening, addressing Ra'd in my heart, *"ya ibni, inta mish mtawel fi hatheh al hayah"* ["Son, you are not long for this life"] … I do not know why I thought that, but I did. And the next day, as was his custom on Thursdays, he went out with his friends from the neighborhood to solicit help for Iraq, which was being attacked by America and the West. Imagine! The whole Western world against Iraq. Ra'd was collecting sugar, rice, blankets, milk – anything for Iraq under attack – but then, who was not collecting for Iraq in those days?"

The question seemed to be an unnecessary diversion for Ahab, and he clucked his tongue at his grandfather, who said: "Go and get us some fruit." Reluctantly, Ahab went off, returning quickly with a bowl full of apples and some knives and small plates on a tray. Abdul Karim went on: "When on Thursday night Ra'd did not return, we went to the mosque to enquire. You see, Doctor, since he was nine or ten years of age, Ra'd, God be pleased with him, was very devout and could recite the Quran and spent much of his time with his friends at the mosque. At the mosque they knew nothing of his whereabouts, but Friday evening we learned from our neighbors of Ra'd's martyrdom ... not death, but martyrdom and entry into eternal Paradise. Later, some of his cousins and relatives told us that they had heard on Radio Monte Carlo of the operation that Ra'd, along with his two friends and neighbors, Ahmad and Radwan, were involved in. It seems that the three friends had been planning this operation for a long time ... they must have had some help, from where I do not know. About 100 kilometers north of Eilat, in Wadi Araba, they attacked a busload of Zionist soldiers ... they attacked over 500 Zionist soldiers with helicopters and sophisticated weapons for six hours before they were martyred. Imagine, three young boys with hardly any training, and with only God's faith in their hearts, engaging the Israeli army for six hours. I do not know how many Israeli soldiers were killed ... some newspapers said 79, others less ... who cares, anyway, the important thing is that Ra'd achieved what he had always talked about – martyrdom in the cause of Palestine.

"Ra'd was born in Amman, he never saw Palestine. Of course, his mother was sad – what mother is not sad at the death, although it was martyrdom, of her son in the spring of his life? He never tasted life, really … he was born in the Hussein refugee camp in Amman …

"The news of his martyrdom spread very quickly. We announced it in the newspapers and opened our house to receive congratulations … it was a feast, not a wake, we prepared coffee and sweets as on feast days … toffee, chocolates, baklava, knafeh … People we knew and even more we did not know came by the thousands to our home for such a martyr's wedding … from Irbid, Maan, Karak, Aqaba, rich and poor alike came to congratulate us on our son's martyrdom. Of course Um Zuhair, his mother, was sad, but she was also very proud and there was no screaming or wailing, just sometimes when a new delegation arrived…

"No, I am not sad … my son died honorably for the cause of Palestine and I like to think that he made a mark."

I too congratulated him and asked if I could hear something about his own life. Where did he come from? How did his son become so involved in religion and politics at the same time? Did he get that from his father?

Abdul Karim was forthcoming in his answers. "I am now, as then when I came from Palestine, forcibly thrown out by the Israelis, a humble man." And then he added, as if it was an afterthought: "None of my children ever saw Palestine, even Zuhair, my eldest, who was born in the mountains and under a tree while we were on the march … no, he was not the eldest, we had a daughter before him, but she died at birth … and now with the death of Ra'd I have only seven sons and two daughters … with Ra'd, I had eight."

Then he laughed and added: "When I left Lod, there was only me, my wife and Zuhair … now between my children and grandchildren we total 39 people, not counting my two daughters and their children … No, I cannot count my daughters and their children along with mine, they belong to their own families.

"It was summer when we left in 1948, the land was planted but not harvested yet … sesame, lentils, grains and vegetables. The first few nights we slept under the skies in the village of Ni'leen, then we moved to Ramallah and then to Aqbat Jabir camp near Jericho, where we remained till 1952. At Aqbat Jabir, UNRWA gave us a tent, the usual rations of flour, sugar, rice, kerosene, etc., and I worked as a bearer, carrying heavy loads on my back – anything to keep skin and bone together – and we survived.

"No, none of my children went to university, except Ra'd, who insisted on studying *Shari'a* [Islamic law] at the University of Damascus. One of my children is still a day laborer and he does well – anyway, better than being a clerk in some office. The rest have trades – electricians, plumbers, and mechanics. As they say, Doctor, a trade provides, although it may not make you rich, and as you see, we live nicely, we now own the four-storey house where my children and I live. We also own a carpentry shop."

It was here that he stopped to ask why I had not brought my wife to visit them. The owner of the laundry next door had apparently told them that she had been with me when I came earlier in the day to find their home. Abdul Karim again ordered tea for us and then added: "As you see, there is not much of a story to tell. I miss Ra'd, but I am proud of him. The Intifada ... if it proved anything, it is that you cannot subjugate a noble people. We Palestinians are a people in jail, but we continue to fight."

One of his sons, Yasin, who had joined us earlier, said: "I cannot understand, Doctor, how they [the Zionists] persist in trying to deny our people their rights. They fight a cruel fight. Since Ra'd's martyrdom I have learned two things: one, that a strong person is strong alone as well as with others ... our family is a religious, not a political one. Ra'd, I know, was touched when Iraq put the phrase *Allahu Akbar*, [God is great] on its flag ... I remember the date, it was 14 January 1991. He and his two friends must have reasoned that they had to leave their own mark. The second thing I became aware of is that only people can be cruel to each other, animals cannot. My brother was a loner who often wondered who would fight for us Palestinians if we do not fight for ourselves. A few days before he went on the operation, he startled me by saying: "You know, Yasin, it is perhaps only in the Arab world that wealth has defeated revolution ... and where so much energy is killed not by others but by our own."

Found among Ra'd's possessions was a letter addressed to his mother, which begins: "Here I am, mother, answering the call, please do not grieve…"

# Epilogue

Tens of thousands of acts of violence and several major battles – 1948, 1956, 1967, and 1973 – have not yet succeeded in resolving the Palestine question. Nor have the several rounds of peace talks that commenced with the Madrid Conference of 1991. One way or another, the war rages on, in words as in deeds; in the bilateral negotiations in Washington; the multilateral negotiations elsewhere in the various capitals of the world. In the south of Lebanon, as well as in the West Bank and the Gaza Strip, the land remains scorched, with the stench of death, gunpowder and human suffering.

For all the Palestinians, like for the people whose stories are related here, the situation not only remains the same, but also seems to deteriorate with time, with Jerusalem still further than the other side of the moon. The dream remains a desert mirage; the stories of the children of the Intifada are a constant reminder to the rest of the world of the struggle of a people yearning to breathe freely.

The breaking of bones and hearts; the demolition of homes; the sealing-off of rooms; the expropriation of land; the deportations, mass and individual; the curfews; the detentions; the prisons and prison camps; the Ansar; the razing of villages; the mushrooming settlements; the arming of settlers; the uprooting not only of the people but of their olive trees, the symbol of peace: the iron fist hammers on.

The stalemate continues, with some Israeli leaders still speaking in an absolutist biblical, ideological fashion. Those who have suffered so much at Nazi and fascist hands mete out similar atrocities to the Palestinians, who have become in Zionist eyes mere insects, objects needing to be cleansed. Not only their national rights and lands but even their very humanity have been expropriated. Neither United Nations resolutions, nor international law nor the normal rules of human behavior seem, thus far, able to induce the Zionists to seriously reconsider their position. The state of Israel, given caesarean birth through the Nazi trauma, continues to terrorize and traumatize the Palestinians.

Hope remains.

*Amman, July 1993*

A priest kneels at the base of an ancient olive tree in the garden of gethsemane Jerusalem, 1967.
© UNRWA Photo by Kay Brennan.

بسم الله الرحمن الرحيم

قال تعالى: (ولا تحسبن الذين قتلوا في سبيل الله أمواتاً بل أحياءً عند ربهم يرزقون)
صدق الله العظيم

عرس شهداء
أل يعقوب (بيت دجن)          أل زيتون ( يافا)
أل الصالحي (اللد)
وعموم أهالي النزهة يزفون إلى الأمة الإسلامية قاطبة، نبأ
استشهاد أبنائهم في العملية البطولية الاستشهادية التي نفذوها
على ثرى فلسطين الطاهر يوم الجمعة الموافق 8/2/91

الشهيد                              الشهيد
مروان عرندس يعقوب              خليل محمود زيتون

الشهيد
رائد عبدالعزيز الصالحي

وأننا أن شاء الله على الطريق الذي سلكتموه لسائرون.
عهداً على الأيام الا تهزموا فالنصر ينبت حيث يرويه الدم.
تقبل التهاني في منازل ذوي الشهداء الكائنة في جبل النزهة /
ضاحية الأمير حسن / قرب مسجد الفالوجة.

Above: Announcement of the martyrdom of three Palestinians which
appeared in the Arab press on 10 February 1991.

Facing page: A translation of the announcement.

138

In the name of God, the Merciful, The Beneficent

*Think not of those who are slain in God's way as dead. Nay, they live, finding their sustenance in the presence of their Lord.*[6]

Wedding of Martyrs

The Ya'kub Family (Beit Dajan), The Zaitun Family (Yafa)
The Salhi Family (Al-Lod)

And all the inhabitants of Nuzha neighborhood declare the good news to the entire Islamic Ummah, of the martyrdom of their children in the heroic operation that they carried out on the hallowed land of Palestine, Friday 8 February 1991.

Martyr                          Martyr
Marwan Arandas Ya'kub          Khalil Mahmoud Zaitoun

Martyr
Ra'd Abdul Aziz al-Salhi

And God willing, we shall follow the same path. And a covenant with time that you shall not be defeated in as much as victory thrives when watered with blood.

Congratulations are accepted at the homes of the families of the martyrs in Jabal al-Nuzhah, Amir Hassan Dahiyyeh, near al-Falujeh Mosque.

---

6. A. Yusuf Ali, *The Holy Quran, Text, Translation and Commentary*, Beirut, Dar al-Arabiyyah Li at-Tiba'ahwa al-NashrWal al-Tawzi

# About the Author

Dr. Kamel S. Abu Jaber (1932–2020) received his PhD from Syracuse University and did a postdoctoral programme in Oriental studies at Princeton University.

Following an academic career in the United States, he returned to Jordan to pursue an extensive academic career as Professor of Political Science and Dean of the College of Economics & Commerce at the University of Jordan. He also assumed a political career becoming Minister of Economy in 1973, Minister of Foreign Affairs in 1991, heading the joint Jordanian-Palestinian delegation to the Madrid Peace Conference. He also served as Senator in the Jordanian Parliament. Other positions include: Director, Jordan University's Center for Strategic Studies; Director, Queen Alia Social Welfare Fund; President, the Jordanian Institute of Diplomacy; President, Higher Council for Media; President, Royal Institute for Interfaith Studies; President, Jordan Institute for Middle Eastern Studies.

An internationally recognised scholar, well known and respected statesman, Dr. Kamel S. Abu Jaber has written many articles and books, among them *The Arab Ba'ath Socialist Party* (1966), *The Jordanians* (1980), *The Palestinians: People of the Olive Tree* (1993) and *Sheepland* (2005).

# About the Artist

Sliman Mansour (born in Birzeit, Palestine in 1947) is a Palestinian painter, illustrator, author and art instructor who has contributed greatly to art promotion and education in the West Bank.

He is regarded as a pivotal cultural leader in Palestine. Co-founder of the Wasiti Art Center in Jerusalem, Mansour's work has been exhibited in Palestine, the United States of America, Japan, Korea and across the Arab world and Europe.